The Which? Guide to
Working from Home

About the author

Lynn Brittney, who has worked in public relations, publishing and as a lecturer, has written articles for various magazines and journals as well as several books. Her other books include a series of Directors' Guides for the Institute of Directors, *Intelligent Manufacturing* (Addison Wesley) and *Successful Conferences and Other Business Events* (WEKA Publishing), and, for Foulsham, *Study Time Management* and *A Woman Alone*. She is the author of *The Which? Guide to Domestic Help*.

The Which? Guide to Working from Home

Lynn Brittney

 CONSUMERS' ASSOCIATION

Which? Books are commissioned and researched by
Consumers' Association and published by
Which? Ltd, 2 Marylebone Road, London NW1 4DF
Email address: books@which.net

Distributed by The Penguin Group:
Penguin Books Ltd, 27 Wrights Lane, London W8 5TZ

First edition October 1994
Revised edition April 1996
Second edition March 1999

British Library Cataloguing in Publication Data
A catalogue record for this book is available from the British Library

ISBN 0 85202 754 0

For a full list of *Which?* books, please write to Which? Books, Castlemead, Gascoyne Way,
Hertford X, SG14 1LH or access our web site at www.which.net

Cover and text design by Kyzen Creative Consultants

Typeset by Saxon Graphics Ltd, Derby
Printed and bound in Great Britain by Clays Ltd, Bungay, Suffolk

Contents

★Please note that you can find in this list the addresses and telephone/fax numbers for all those organisations marked with an asterisk in the text

Introduction

Working from home is a positive choice being made by more and more people each year. Some people do it because they are starting up a new business and do not want separate premises until they have a going concern. Others, perhaps with small or not-so-small children, just want to work as many or as few hours as suits them. A growing number are employees of companies that, in today's task-oriented business environment, depend on teleworkers to provide them with a flexible workforce. Many are self-employed people who have left commuting behind them to re-purpose their skills. Some are not fully mobile and therefore cannot easily travel to a workplace outside the home. Yet others work from home because the property itself provides a source of income.

This guide provides an entrée for all these sections of the workforce, alerting them to the pitfalls as well as the advantages of being a home-based worker.

In recent years, various laws and regulations have been passed which affect the way in which people can work from home. These include the National Minimum Wage (for those who employ staff or work at home themselves for a company) and the Working Time Directive, which limits the number of hours employees may work each week. These are developments of which both employees and employers need to be aware, and which are explained in the course of this book.

Advances in information and communications technology have made working from home a far more practical and viable option for many thousands of people than it was in the past, reducing issues such as location and distance from employer base to mere detail. The EU expects that Europe alone will be accommodating about 10 million teleworkers by the year 2000. At the time of writing, in late1998, the UK has roughly 1,150,000 teleworkers – employed, self-employed and 'occasional'. By early 2000 this figure is expected to increase to 4 million.

Even the government has recognised the trend, and is supporting it. A 1998 booklet issued by the DTI and entitled *Working Anywhere* states that:

> The Government wants to help people strike the right balance between their work and home lives. Working different or shorter hours, perhaps from the convenience of home or from a local workplace, can help parents balance work with the pleasures and responsibilities of bringing up a family. Both women and men can gain from this sort of flexibility, provided that the new working methods are appropriate and introduced by consent . . . New technologies offer us the possibility to change our working practices for the better.

For those who retire early – a rapidly expanding element of society – working at home, having left behind the daily grind of travelling to a place of employment, can be an ideal solution. Active, fit and highly experienced, those in their 50s and 60s who wish to continue some sort of income-generating occupation will find a range of possibilities open to them. Many enrol at colleges throughout the UK to prepare themselves for second careers which they can pursue from home: garden landscaping, chiropody, computer support and vehicle maintenance are just a few examples.

As recession and widespread unemployment loom once again, the entrepreneurial spirit plays an ever greater role in the economic life of the country. Despite the mounting pressures of legislation, the numbers of innovators prepared to take the risk of setting up a new small business show little sign of diminishing – from agencies supplying childcare and eldercare services to individuals making high-value hand-crafted goods on a small scale, or teaching languages, music or how to make sushi, or retired couples converting their homes for bed and breakfast. Ideas exist in plenty, but harnessing them to the right practices, checking out the rules and regulations that might govern your chosen area of endeavour, and marketing your skills, services or goods, can sometimes require a little help and support.

That is where this book comes in. It may not have all the answers to all the questions, but it can certainly point you in the right direction.

Chapter 1

Working from home

Each year, a significant proportion of the working population elects to become self-employed or start up a small business. These people have opted to escape from the traditional role of the employee and many of them make the home their working environment. The statistics vary as to exactly how many people work from home. Government sources from the early 1990s estimated that by 1996 over five million people, both employed and self-employed, would be working from home. This would seem to have underestimated the way in which certain sectors of the home-based working industry have expanded. For example, research by Henley Business School in 1997 stated that there were at least four million teleworkers in the UK – people who spend at least half of their working week at home using telecommunications and computer technology to do their job. The 1997 *UK Labour Force Survey* showed that, in the first quarter of that year, there were 987,000 teleworkers in Britain, who were employees of companies, most of which were in the insurance, banking and finance sectors. These figures, of course, do not include all the other individuals who work from home, either as lone entrepreneurs or running small home-based businesses. The Department of Trade and Industry (DTI) estimates that there are about four million small businesses in the UK in 1998, but is unable to give a breakdown of how many of these are actually home-based. Another government survey carried out in 1997 gives a figure of 1.1 million people working from home. So, although the statistics are confusing they all seem to point to one thing – working from home is a choice that a growing number of individuals and companies have made.

Sadly, a large proportion of small businesses fail each year, but various sources report that these statistics seem to relate to the businesses that have expanded beyond the one-man/woman band and out of using the home as a base. Perhaps the greater risks involved in paying for working premises and employing staff often contribute to the demise of small companies. A healthy percentage of people seem to survive self-employment and continue to have happy and profitable careers. And those who survive expansion into a fully fledged business do so because each step of the way is planned and built into the balance sheet from the beginning – something that is discussed later in this chapter.

Working for others

The self-employed and teleworkers are not the only people working from home; there are also thousands of homeworkers, skilled and unskilled, who are employed by someone else. Statistics are patchy on this section of the working community, mainly because few representative bodies are interested in the conditions and contracts under which homeworkers operate. Those that are may be concerned with only a certain section of the homeworking community; for example there are five Low Pay Units in existence in the UK which were set up to advise upon and monitor the employment of homeworkers, many of whom are women from ethnic communities.

Changes in society and the job market

Until recent years, those who worked from home were either generating a second income (e.g. a wife who had developed a hobby into a paying concern) or people who were, by reason of disability or family commitments, confined to the home and the limited work opportunities on offer. However, the recession of the early 1990s and the resultant drastic changes in the job market have created a new generation of people who earn money at home. A large proportion of these are the sole breadwinners in their family who have to make their home-based occupation produce sufficient money to meet all their bills.

Rising divorce statistics have meant that there are more single parents who are turning to home-based occupations which provide extra money while allowing them to continue to be an active parent. And a more recent development is that of the early retiree who gives up full-time work in his or her fifties and needs an occupation which will provide continued stimulation as well as bring in revenue. Often, early retirement provides an excellent opportunity for someone to develop a totally new home-based profession. Many colleges which run training courses for alternative therapy practitioners, for example, have reported an increasing number of mature students in their fifties.

Less fortunate are those who are made redundant in mid-life and find the job market has closed ranks against them. For such people, retraining or developing an existing skill into a home-based business can be a lifesaver.

A world of employment options

Continuing unemployment and the expansion in numbers of early retirees and active pensioners have had the result that anyone considering embarking upon self-employment today has an unprecedented number of training schemes, diploma courses and business courses on offer, a large percentage of which are available during the day as opposed to the evenings.

Other developments in the market-place have enabled many people to start working for themselves in a small way. Franchising, developed in the USA in the 1960s and 1970s, has taken quite a hold in the UK, with some 568 business format franchises in the UK who are members of the British Franchise Association (BFA).* Franchising, as defined by the BFA, is 'a market-orientated method of distribution in which one person, the Franchisor, grants a licence or a franchise to another person, the Franchisee, which permits the Franchisee to use the Franchisor's trade name, trade marks and business system in return for an initial payment and further regular payment.' In other words, one buys the right to operate a proven service or business in the manner approved by the parent company. Many of these franchises are very big operations indeed, but some are one-man/woman operations, such as carpet and upholstery

CASE HISTORY: Peter

Peter is a retired accountant in his early sixties who was formerly employed by a large firm of accountants in Bradford. When he retired he was financially very secure but was bored and frustrated by not having any work to do. At his daughter's suggestion he visited a franchise exhibition and found several one-man/woman franchises that appealed to him. Being an accountant he was able to investigate the financial viability of the various proposals and he took professional advice from his bank's franchise department and a friend in a marketing consultancy. He then purchased a printing franchise which specialises in printing business stationery and so on and which he could operate from home. It has proved so successful that he now employs his daughter and one other member of staff.

cleaning systems, mobile fast-food outlets and business services, to name but a few. Franchising is attracting a great deal of interest. The BFA reports that, since the establishment of its web site in April 1998, some 3,000 visitors a week have been tapping into the latest news and information on franchising.

Also on the increase are 'network marketing' schemes, also called 'multi-level selling' (formerly called 'pyramid selling'). Network marketing is a method of selling goods or services to the general public – usually door to door, or to individuals or through 'parties' (a gathering of friends or neighbours). These goods or services are purchased by the participants from a central source or from other participants in the 'pyramid' or 'network'. Participants not only make commissions on the sales that they personally generate but also on the sales of any other 'agents' they have recruited. These multi-level marketing schemes acquired a bad reputation and caused the government to legislate to protect participants. The Pyramid Selling Regulations 1989 and the Pyramid Selling Schemes (Amendment) Regulations 1990 are both part of the Third Trading Act 1973. As a result of this legislation some very fair network marketing schemes are now in existence and it is possible to make a reasonable income from them. However, caution should still be exercised. Often unscrupulous companies who offer 'get rich quick' schemes are only seeking to offload stock. In China net-

---

CASE HISTORY: Patrick

Patrick is a consultant engineer. He was working for a very large consultancy in Central London but found that he was spending a great deal of time commuting and was also working on projects which he did not feel he was best suited to manage. He began to make enquiries among his contacts and discovered that there was a place in the freelance market-place for his particular skills. He drew up a business plan and managed to secure a bank loan to equip his home office with the necessary technology and to have brochures printed. The loan was made easier by the fact that he had managed to capture a contract with a large company before officially starting up. He now earns more than he did as an employee and he is able to work mainly in the field of petro-chemicals, which interests him most.

---

work marketing is now illegal, thousands of people having lost their life savings through their involvement with such companies. Further details on choosing a reputable network marketing scheme are explored in Chapter 2.

Restrictions on enterprise

Anyone earning money at home today has to face the fact that legislation imposes more restrictions than ever on the budding entrepreneur. Even the earner of modest 'pin money' who makes jam and cakes to sell at bazaars has to meet a barrage of food regulations designed to ensure maximum food safety and hygiene for the buying public.

Banks, unfortunately, are far less inclined today to lend money to assist business start-ups than they were ten years ago. Much of the grant aid that was on offer in certain areas for developing industries has dried up. However, loan facilities may be available, see Chapter 5.

Despite all that, the picture is not gloomy: sources of finance do exist, and the legislation can be coped with. Good, relatively well-paid homework is available country-wide. Large technology-based companies are finding it increasingly attractive to employ teleworkers as it is one way of cutting down their overheads.

CASE HISTORY: Sharon

Sharon is a young mother with one baby. Money is a bit tight and she needed to get some sort of job. However, she has no relatives who can look after her baby and when she investigated the cost of nursery care in her area she realised that if she worked full-time in a shop she would barely be able to make enough money to pay for her baby to be looked after, let alone make some extra money to pay bills. She saw an advertisement in the local paper for homeworkers and when she telephoned the number given was told that the work was packing greetings cards. Sharon took the job and has found that in a good week she can make about £68, which pays a few of the bills. The work is repetitive but not unpleasant; she can do quite a lot in the evenings while watching television, and sometimes her husband helps. The company requested that she should be self-employed and therefore take care of her own tax and National Insurance. Because of her low earnings she has not yet paid tax but she voluntarily pays Class 2 NI.

Why work from home?

The reasons why people choose to work from home are as diverse as the ways they choose to earn their money. For some, the desire to opt out of the rat race, the pressures of daily commuting, the personality clashes in the office or factory take precedence over the security of a monthly salary cheque. The tradition of staying in a job 'man and boy' is virtually moribund, and this, combined with the growing popularity and success of working from home will profoundly affect the way in which people view their jobs in the future.

A first analysis of the motives for earning money from home may point to ultimate success or failure. If, for example, the prime motive for working at home is so that you can have more free time, this could point to a lack of the self-discipline that any self-employed person needs by the spadeful.

Typical reasons why people work from home are:

• they have small children, need some extra income, but do not wish to leave the home to work

- they have small children and cannot afford nursery care
- they have no means of transport and commuting to work would be difficult
- they are disabled and either housebound or unable to find employment out of the home
- they manufacture products, in a small way, in their home and have always done so; to rent extra premises would be expensive
- they can save three hours a day by not travelling to and from a job – this means they can see more of their family and save travel costs
- they cannot get a job on the open market because of age, lack of qualifications or other factors
- they have an illness which, although it does not totally disable them, restricts the number of hours they can work or gives them 'good' days and 'bad' days
- they have skills that can be easily practised from home, for example book-keeping or dressmaking

CASE HISTORY: Norman

Norman was made redundant in his late forties and, after eight months of unsuccessful job-hunting, decided to use his redundancy money to train as a driving instructor and to buy an adapted car. He now runs his own one-man driving school from his home. The demand has proved so high locally that his wife is undergoing similar training so that she can come into the business.

CASE HISTORY: Barry

Barry is paraplegic and, although he is a qualified teacher, finds the demands of daily school life too great. He decided to set up at home as a private tutor in maths and has a full client list. The pupils come to him for their lessons, and most of his work is in the early evenings and at weekends. He also makes extra income by invigilating at examinations and marking the papers.

CASE HISTORY: Marion

Marion is a middle-aged housewife whose children are in their late teens. Her husband earns a good salary and their mortgage is paid off, so Marion has no need to work but wants to have some independence.

It has been nineteen years since Marion worked in a clerical job and she has had no training for any other work. She decided to take an evening class in basic computer skills so that she could learn to use her son's computer. This was so enjoyable that she graduated from the basic course to the more specialist software courses. She then began to look around the job market but decided that she really wanted to work from home so that she could continue to enjoy her garden and be with her family. A friend put her in touch with a publishing house and she is now employed to key in book manuscripts on to computer disks which are then passed on to the typesetters. She does about four hours' work a day, which leaves her free for the rest of the day to care for her house and garden and enjoy other activities.

- they want an interest in life which will provide some income but also allows them time to devote to family and home
- they are members of that fortunate section of the working community who can earn more money working for themselves, using their home as a base, than they can working for an employer, for example builders, consultants and so on.

The advantages

There are many advantages to working from home, depending upon your chosen occupation and your personality.

- **It is cheap** You save a considerable amount of money by not travelling to your place of work and, if you are self-employed, by not having to rent or buy other premises.
- **There are tax benefits** By using part of your own home for work you are allowed to claim part of the costs of the mortgage or rent, heating, lighting and telephone. Any alterations or repairs done to the premises which are directly related to

improving your working conditions can also be put through your accounts.

- **It saves time** The hours that you would otherwise spend in travelling can be devoted to work.
- **It is flexible** If you are a parent, you can take advantage of certain types of work that can be fitted into the school hours. If you have pre-school children you may be able to work when they are in bed in the evening. Alternatively, you may just want to work unconventional hours because they suit you better; if you function best in the mornings you can start work early and finish early or, if you are a night owl, you can work late. The flexibility of working hours obviously depends upon the type of occupation and whether it relies upon interaction with people who work normal office hours. The self-employed insurance salesman may find that he or she has to make all his or her calls in the evening because that is when most working people are at home. The craft worker or writer may be able to work any hour of the day or night, whereas a mobile hairdresser may find that his or her clients demand appointments during the daytime only.
- **It is comfortable** Working in your own home can be relaxing. You can wear whatever you like, you have control over your environment – the temperature, the lighting, the décor. You can drink as many cups of tea and coffee as you like and when you like, and time your breaks to suit yourself.
- **You see more of your family** No more being a weekend parent because you are usually on your way to work when the kids get up and you don't get back until they are in bed.

CASE HISTORY: Eric

Eric took early retirement at the age of 57 and decided to develop his hobby, carpentry, into a modest business. He now makes wooden children's toys which he sells at craft fairs, and this generates welcome extra income. He has no desire to develop the business further and is content with just occupying his spare time. His wife often runs the craft fair stalls as she enjoys the friendly atmosphere and the marketing side of the business.

CASE HISTORY: Hilary

Hilary is a single parent of two school-age children. Although she receives adequate maintenance from her ex-husband she felt that she needed to generate some extra money, but did not want to go out to work and have her children looked after by someone else after school hours. Her greatest love has always been cooking, and she has a Cordon Bleu diploma which she gained before her marriage. She decided that she could put this skill to use during school hours and hit upon the idea of business lunches. She approached all the local businesses and offered a boardroom luncheon service. Her own kitchen was inspected and approved by the local Environmental Health Department so that she could prepare the food there and transport it to the clients. For those offices that do not have any means of heating food she uses a variety of portable methods – slo-cookers, small microwaves, electric rings and so on. She prepares anything from sandwiches and salads to full Cordon Bleu meals.

- **You can have family support** It may be possible to enlist the help of those members of your family who have the time to assist you to get tasks completed, for example, a parent or teenage children, who might be available at weekends to help.
- **You can work at your own pace** From the start you can decide just how much work you want to take on. You may simply be trying to generate a little extra money for your family rather than providing the main income. You may be disabled or ill and so only capable of coping with a certain amount of concentrated physical or mental effort. You may be an early retiree or a pensioner who just wants an occupation to fill in the spare time, or your whole lifestyle may depend upon you making a go of self-employment and therefore you are prepared to work every hour there is in order to make a success of things. Whatever your situation, you now have the choice – you can run your working life.

The disadvantages

- **Restrictions** There could be restrictions that prevent you from using your home as a base for business. If you have a quiet and unobtrusive occupation such as hand-knitting or book-binding this may not be classified as a 'business' under the terms of whatever contract covers your residence. However, when an occupation substantially encroaches on the domestic use of a house – say a mail-order business for which half the house is filled with boxes and packages, a carpentry workshop in the basement filled with flammable materials, wood and chemicals, or a motorbike repair service which litters up your front and back garden and garage with dismantled bikes, then your building society or landlord and, certainly, your insurer will take a dim view of such proceedings. Before starting on any venture you should check the details of all leases, deeds, charges and covenants to see whether running a business in your home is prohibited. Similarly, local bylaws may prohibit any occupations which involve a fire risk, noisy machinery or frequent deliveries by large vehicles.

- **You may need planning permission** This is required if your home-based occupation changes the use of a building, for example converting your living room into a tea shop, using two rooms in your house as a waiting room and treatment room, or turning your garden into a cattery.

  There is a general rule that if you are using less than half your house as office space, or your shed as a workshop, then you do not have to apply for planning permission. However, this rule is not hard and fast. The key to it all is unobtrusiveness. You could run a very small office from one room in your house without any problem, but if you suddenly started receiving frequent visits from customers who parked their cars outside and prevented residents from parking in a residential area you could find yourself falling foul of the local authority.

  Check with the local authority before starting your new venture because they will be concerned not just over change of use of a house but also whether your business will contribute to noise or air pollution, whether you are planning any structural alterations to your house and whether your activities come under the scrutiny of the department concerned with health and safety.

- **You will need extra insurance** Your home contents policy will certainly have to be extended to cover your work materials, records and also outbuildings if you are using them for storage or as workshops. You may need to consider other forms of insurance – public liability, professional indemnity (see Chapter 6) and some form of private health insurance and pension.

- **You need to pay greater attention to home security** If your whole livelihood is housed in your home you cannot afford to be burgled. You may have high-value, easily portable equipment such as computers, fax machines, specialist tools and so on. You may work with valuable materials such as gold and silver. You will almost certainly have to use your home address, or at least your telephone number, in advertising and publicity, even if only on business cards. This, unfortunately, does make your home a target.

  Outbuildings, of course, are at greater risk. You need to make the garden and the buildings as secure as possible. It is best to seek advice on this from the local police.

- **You may be too easily distracted at home** If the work that you are doing requires great concentration you may find working in a home environment is too noisy, family life is too intrusive, or you are too easily tempted to break off from work and do other things.

- **You may get lonely** If you do not have a family, or the family are out at work all day, you may find the solitude of working at home unbearable. If you are engaged in some sort of craft work which is easily portable, you may find that the answer is to team up with like-minded people in your area and work together in each other's houses.

- **It could adversely affect your family life** Because you cannot leave the pressures of work at an office and calm down on the way home, or expect your children to talk in whispers all day or your partner to refrain from using noisy household appliances, resentments may build up on both sides. You have to be sure that you have a personality that can adapt to working at home. You may have decided to pursue an occupation which is home-based but, in fact, gets you out and about most of the time, in which case conflict between you and the family should not arise. But people who have sedentary home-based jobs need to be self-disciplined yet relaxed, able to work as many hours as needed, then shut work off and give the family some time too. It is not an easy juggling act.

- **Working for yourself can mean insecurity** Will enough money come in to pay next month's bills? Will customers pay on time or will you have to chase them? Can you get the work done on time? Will the demand for your product or service continue? These questions will probably occupy a good deal of your attention from time to time. If you are a second-income generator the pressure may not be so great, but many people find that coping with the cash-flow worries of self-employment can be too much.

- **Working for someone else can also mean insecurity** Homeworkers rarely have the sort of contracts that offer some sort of compensation if their services are no longer required. It is always best not to put all your eggs in one basket. Have one or two sources of part-time work on the go at once, so that if one fails you can perhaps increase the hours on another, without too much loss of income.

- **Working for someone else can sometimes mean boring and poorly paid work** The work may be easy and possible to do while watching television but it may be tiring and pay very little. Do you have the patience to stuff envelopes all day long? Or sew millions of buttons on clothes? Your home may also be cluttered with dozens of boxes or bags of work waiting to be done. You may have to process thousands of pieces a week to make a living wage. This type of work can be very repetitive and time-consuming.

- **You may only be earning a commission and do long hours of work for no return at all** There are home-based jobs, such as telephone canvassing, where the employee has the telephone bill paid but only earns commission on successful conversions into sales. This can mean making hundreds of telephone calls (sometimes receiving abuse from the people you are calling) without earning anything at all.

- **You may have to traipse the street in all weathers, delivering and collecting catalogues, orders, directories or leaflets** Many network-marketing schemes involve delivering catalogues to houses over quite large areas and then knocking on doors to get them back a few days later, with orders if you are lucky. Some people deliver phone directories, local newspapers or leaflets. Others do house-to-house surveys. All these jobs have to be done whatever the weather, and, quite often, during the evenings.

- **Your work could be dangerous** Collecting money door-to-door for football pools, Christmas clubs, debt collectors or catalogues can be hazardous. Walking the streets at a regular time each week with large amounts of cash on your person is an invitation to muggers.

Preparation is the key to success

Once you have analysed your motives for working from home and weighed up the advantages and disadvantages, you are halfway to preparing yourself for a fruitful and satisfying working life.

Every business should work out a business plan before starting up to make sure that every possible eventuality is covered in its scheme of operation for the first few years. If you are contemplating earning money from home, however modestly, you should do the same thing. You must analyse every step you plan to take in the future and prepare yourself for any direction in which your chosen occupation may take you.

This may seem unnecessary at first – after all, you're only decorating a few wedding cakes for your friends, aren't you? But what happens if one of your wedding cakes is so admired by a professional baker that he or she offers you a contract to decorate fifty cakes a week? You can't resist the money, the challenge and the security but suddenly you are catapulted from a paying hobby into a small business. You hadn't planned on it; you didn't actively market yourself, it just happened. Without preparation you are lost – the effort of meeting the orders leaves you no time to sort out accounts, get some back-up help and deal with the authorities if necessary.

If you had investigated every possible business scenario before you even started your venture, gathered the information needed for possible expansion and sorted out a fail-safe mechanism should things go wrong, then you would have laid the foundations for success or, at the very least, a painless withdrawal from something that did not work out as you had hoped.

What if . . . ?

This is the question you should ask yourself at the preparation stage and then discuss the answers with your family, friends, investors or advisors.

What if . . .

- **No one wants my product or services?** Have you researched the market-place to gauge demand? Can you adapt your product or service in some way to appeal to a different market sector? Can you diversify and provide something else using the same materials/skills?

- **I can't make enough money from each piece of work to make a profit?** Perhaps you are concentrating on items that are too expensive and too time-consuming. If the market is not there, can you produce smaller, cheaper items that are less labour-intensive and have a higher profit margin? Would you make more money if you offered your skills for part of the process rather than for all of it? Or would it be still more profitable to write about or teach your skill rather than practising it?

- **I get more work than I can handle?** This is where the preparation comes in handy. You have to set up a back-up infrastructure at the beginning. This may be no more than getting to know people in your area with similar or related skills, finding out their availability and discussing with them the possibility that you may need their help at some time in the future and that you would be willing to reciprocate.

  Before you start up you can decide, as a family, which members would be available, capable and interested enough to help you if the orders came thick and fast. You may have friends who would be able to help you now and then on a part-time basis – several part-time helpers add up to at least two full-time pairs of hands.

  Of course, in order to pay for extra help you will have to take a cut in profit and perhaps adjust your price structure to customers. This also has to be planned ahead; many rapidly expanding companies get caught off-guard when they are suddenly offered a large contract and grab it too quickly without adjusting prices first to allow for the employment of extra staff.

- **I get sick?** Again, you need to have back-up mechanisms set in place wherever possible to take care of the business side of things. On the personal side, however, it is a matter of adequate insurance cover. If you want to protect yourself (and your family) from loss of your income as a result of illness or death, consider topping up your life insurance and taking out permanent health insurance and perhaps critical illness insurance. You could also consider private medical insurance which would give you some control over the timing of an operation, so that you could either speed up the time it would take to get treated or organise it to coincide with a slack business period. You may also want to consider what is known as 'key person' insurance which can cover you against any business losses incurred by accident or unforeseen ill-health.

- **My children get sick and I can't work because I am looking after them?** This depends on the economics of your business. How much money will you lose if you look after them yourself? In the early stages of your enterprise, probably not much. However, if you have a deadline to meet, or a new contract that is worth a lot of money to you, perhaps you can have grandparents to stay for the period of the illness or you can pay a friend to child-sit while his or her own children are at school. If this scenario is discussed with the parties concerned at a very early stage in your venture you will know that you have their agreement in principle and it is not something you have to worry about. (Those with live-in or live-out nannies for pre-school children won't have to worry anyway.) If things are really extreme – you have no available grandparents or friends to bale you out – then, if the finances can stand it and the work is that important, you could always hire an agency nurse for a week. After all, you will be in the house yourself, albeit shut away in another room, and available if there are problems.

- **I need more equipment?** If you can, budget at the beginning for future expansion. If you cannot put money away you will have to borrow the money to buy equipment outright, or investigate leasing or hire terms. Talk to your bank at the beginning – you will need to show them some sort of business plan and discuss what they may be able to offer you in the future and what they will charge for loans or overdraft facilities. Obtain information from the equipment manufacturers or hire centres – you may find that it works out cheaper to lease than to have a bank loan. But make all the enquiries at the beginning so that you know what your future outgoings are likely to be.

- **I need more space to cope with increased business?** Again, talk it over with your family, local authority and neighbours long before you ever need to do anything. Could you afford to build an extension to your house? You can even go through the whole process of drawing up plans and getting planning permission – the permission is valid for five years before it has to be resubmitted. But do discuss it with neighbours; it may be that they would object to any planned extension. It may also be the case that the local authority would refuse planning permission. If you investigate all these things at the outset you may discover that at a certain point in your business expansion you will either have to rent space outside the home, move to a bigger house, convert the cellar or loft or move your work into a very large garden shed.

- **Customers won't pay their bills?** First, you have to be very strict about payment terms, invoicing and following up invoices. Don't do commissioned work such as a wedding dress, a painting or a piece of furniture on credit; ask for payments along the way. Find out what your local solicitor will charge for sending intimidating letters to bad payers – some solicitors now offer a cheap service for this. Make a resolution, from the beginning, that if anyone defaults on a bill more than twice you will no longer carry out work for them. If all else fails you can go to a factoring company or a specialist debt-collecting agency. They will undertake to collect the monies owed to you in return for a percentage.

- **Employers don't pay me?** Make sure at the outset that you don't get a job with one of the blacklisted companies that have a reputation for very low pay and defaulting on wages. Various organisations can advise you on this (see Chapter 3). Once an employer has defaulted, the first thing is to find out why. If it is because of bankruptcy you will be contacted by the Official Receiver and asked to put in your bid for monies owed to you. If it is for some other reason, you may need the advice of ACAS★ and perhaps a solicitor. It is best to know your rights before seeking home employment.

Ready to start?

No! Preparation is essential before you start to earn money from home. Choose your line of work, then do your market research. Next, you have to sort out your finances – start-up costs, running costs, banking and accounting methods. The following chapter will set you on the right path – read on!

Chapter 2

What can you do?

Having analysed your motives, needs and personality you have decided that you are suited to working from home. You may, of course, already know what you want to do, or you may have absolutely no idea. It's worthwhile looking at the options.

CASE HISTORY: David

David works for a large entertainment organisation in their computer section. His job was to amend the huge mailing list that was held on computer. David's section of the organisation was sold to another group and some of the workforce were offered the chance to work from home. David has a young family and he relished the chance to spend more time with them, so he opted for the teleworker offer. His salary was decreased slightly but this was offset by the fact that he no longer had to pay fares. All his other benefits – pension, medical insurance and so on – stay the same. Because he is an employee, the computer hardware and modem belong to his employers and his contract forbids him to use them to do any other work or to introduce any unauthorised software or disks because of the risk of viruses. He works from 9a.m. until 3.30p.m., which exactly coincides with his children's school hours. The job is working out so well that David's wife is considering getting a part-time job because David is able to take the children to school, fetch them home and look after them.

Translate an existing job into a home-based one

Many teleworkers have done just that. Their employers have allowed them to contribute to the corporate workload from their home base. This is an ideal scenario because you are doing a job which obviously suits you very well in terms of skills and aptitude and you are still an employee, with the attendant financial security. However, only a very small percentage of the population can take advantage of such an option.

With the technological explosion of the Internet, it has become possible for those who have the appropriate skills to go freelance and use their knowledge to set up a home-based business or consultancy. The Internet and electronic mail (email) have become powerful business tools for finding and distributing information, advertising, selling products and services and conducting business globally without the need to step outside your front door.

You may be happy doing your current job but not happy to be an employee. Many consultants simply leave full-time employment and opt for home-based self-employment. Provided they have done the market research first and made the necessary contacts to ensure a regular supply of work, the transition from office working to home working can be problem-free.

Other professions whose practitioners can easily set up at home include hairdressers, beauticians, masseurs, chiropodists and upholsterers, for example. All can offer a visiting service to clients in their own homes or have clients come to them.

Translate existing employment knowledge into your own venture

Many people who have worked for years in particular industries find that now, with the aid and support of computer technology they can set up their own business or consultancy at home, using the knowledge they have gained over many years. Publishing, for example. It is possible now to become a modestly successful one-man/woman publisher of books, pamphlets and magazines at home by using desk-top packages to create professional products.

Teaching from home has become a popular option for retired or disabled teachers who have a thorough knowledge of the National Curriculum and can offer specialist tuition. Some people now run their own small agencies from home, capitalising on expertise gained when in the employ of large agencies. These agencies offer anything from domestic staff to travel or public relations.

Develop new skills by training part-time

This is a popular route to a new career for people who are approaching retirement and for anyone who is returning to the job market. Many younger people, bored and frustrated in full-time employment that does not offer any stimulation, have also turned to adult education classes to provide them with new qualifications to restart a career.

Training does not have to be lengthy or demanding – it is possible to acquire certain skills, provided one has a talent for them, in just a few months. Cake decorating, picture framing and keyboard skills are examples.

Sometimes people are already highly skilled in certain areas but feel that they need the appropriate diplomas or certificates to give extra confidence to their customers. In this case it may be possible, by arrangement with the local adult education institute, just to sit the examinations. Provided you can satisfy the principal of the institute that you are skilled in the relevant field (perhaps by producing testimonials from past employers) there should be no problem. The range and diversity of courses (part-time, day release, evening classes) on offer is surprising. Below is an example of courses at a college in south-east England:

Access courses (for mature students):
Computing
    Healthcare
    Law
    Environmental Science
    Social Sciences
    Teaching
Open Learning (Correspondence):
    Direct Care NVQ

RSA Practical Book-Keeping
Chartered Association of Certified Accountants Foundation
    Stage
Certificate Stage
Building Crafts: Bench Joinery/Carpentry and Joinery NVQ Level
    2 & 3
    Bricklaying
    Electrical Installation
    Painting & Decorating Special Skills
    Plumbing
Building & Civil Engineering
Business Management
Accounting & Insurance
Office Skills
Caring & Education
Counselling
Teaching & Training
Catering & Hospitality
Customer Service
Computing & IT
Engineering & Science
Floral Design & Creative Arts
Hair Design
Holistic Therapies
Social Sciences
Health & Safety
Travel & Tourism
Sport & Fitness

Develop an interest into a service

Some popular money-making ventures do not require any particular skills, just a keen interest in the subject. Many people who love
animals and children begin a profitable home-based career by pet-
sitting or baby-sitting. Looking after pets or children for a short
period in their own homes requires no qualifications. Take note,
however, that if you were to open a kennel or cattery in your garden
or take children into your home every day you would have to be
registered with the appropriate authorities.

CASE HISTORY: Anne

Anne is approaching early retirement at the age of 57 and she feels that she does not want to give up a working life, although she will be financially secure. For the last two years she has been attending a part-time course in horticulture with the intention of becoming a garden designer when she finally retires from her full-time job. Already an avid gardener with an extensive knowledge of horticulture, she nevertheless wants to get the formal qualifications in order to inspire her future customers with confidence.

CASE HISTORY: Matthew

Matthew has been interested in genealogy all his life and has done volunteer research work for various people since he was a teenager. He knows his way so well around the Public Record Office in Kew that someone
recommended him to an American writer who needed to do some research in England but did not have the time. Matthew enjoyed the work and was quite well paid, so he decided to advertise his availability as a researcher in various publications. The response was very encouraging and he is now a full-time researcher of English social history.

A love of libraries, a familiarity with library systems and an interest in certain topics have led many people to offer their services as researchers for authors and academics. No particular qualifications need to be obtained by a would-be researcher other than an extensive knowledge of a particular subject matter and the ability to locate the necessary sources of information.

Gardening is one area where many people have made an interest into a profitable career. No one asks the jobbing gardener whether he or she has trained at a horticultural college. Someone who sets themselves up as a garden designer or offers landscaping services or tree surgery, though, will find that customers are likely to be a little more particular.

Develop a hobby into a business

It is not unusual to make a hobby pay in some small way, even if you have no intention of turning it into a business. Materials are so expensive nowadays that very few people can afford to, say, make picture frames or small pieces of furniture without occasionally offering them up for sale so that they can afford to buy new materials.

Sometimes skilled hobbyists are spurred along the road to self-employment by donating a piece of work to a charitable sale and being surprised by how quickly and profitably it sells. Why not sell it themselves? Then the appraisal has to be done regarding the demand for the work, the price the customer is prepared to pay and how much, in reality, when time, labour and materials are properly costed, the work is actually worth. Sadly, many beautiful crafts are greatly undervalued when one considers the time and effort that are put into them. However, the materials may not be expensive and although you should always approach self-employment with the intention of making enough money to cover all overheads, you cannot strictly apply the rule if you are a second-income generator with a great love for your craft work. Satisfaction is worth a great deal in life and, as one happy and fulfilled needlewoman says, 'I regard my little "business" as therapy that pays for itself!'

CASE HISTORY: Stanley

Stanley's lifelong hobby has been breeding budgerigars and his birds have won many awards in shows. Various people at the shows kept asking him if they could buy some of his birds and, eventually, he decided to make this a full-time job. He sells the birds through the hobby magazine and to reputable pet shops and garden centres (which he personally inspects). He also writes articles on the subject and has just finished his first book.

Do unskilled work at home for someone else

This may be the only option open to you at the moment if you have no skills or hobbies to develop nor the time to train for a new career.

Many of the people who work at home for an outside employer are doing the type of work generally done in a factory, assembling anything from watch straps to fire extinguishers, making toys or lampshades, filling Christmas crackers, finishing textile products. A lot of such work is done for the clothing industry. Much of the work is repetitive, requires little skill (but attention) and does not lead to the satisfaction of seeing the finished product.

Finding such work and ensuring that you are getting a fair deal is not easy. It has to be approached with some caution and it is best to be aware of possible pitfalls before answering advertisements for unskilled homework (see Chapter 3).

Do skilled work at home for someone else

This is a more promising line of work to pursue, because if you have a skill that is in demand you will be paid a reasonable rate by an employer.

This type of work may be more difficult to find and may require some marketing on your part. For example, if you are a skilled hand – or machine – knitter but you do not want the insecurity or the hassle of working for yourself you may have to approach local wool shops, haberdashers or clothes shops to see if they would be interested in paying you for garments.

CASE HISTORY: Donald

Donald is an unskilled homeworker. He is mentally handicapped and cannot easily find a job. However, his mother answered an advertisement for homeworkers in the local paper and found that the work was simple, consisting of filling Christmas crackers with paper hats, mottoes and toys. Donald quite enjoys this work and has become good at it. It doesn't pay very much but it is enough to give him some independence.

CASE HISTORY: Sandra

Sandra is a skilled homeworker. She hand-knits beautiful Fair Isle sweaters for a Scottish company which sells them mainly through tourist shops in Scotland and abroad. She has actually seen some of her sweaters in a Scottish shop in an international airport. Sandra got the job because she lives near the company and she was able to show them some samples of her knitting. She is a fast worker and is paid a good rate for the sweaters, which sell for quite a high price. The company supplies the wool and specifies the pattern she is to knit. She enjoys the work and knits five days a week for a good eight hours in between the hours of 10a.m. and 10p.m., with frequent breaks.

Wool manufacturers are always looking for skilled knitters, but bear in mind that there are only a handful of manufacturers and many thousands of good knitters.

People in the Scottish Highlands and Islands have, of course, been homeworkers or outworkers for centuries, producing sweaters, tartan cloth and so on for clothing manufacturers who pay them by the piece. Many clothing manufacturers employ home-workers to sew small parts of garments together or to finish or inspect them. Most employers are honest and fair but the textile and clothing industries have borne a bad reputation in the past for taking advantage of homeworkers.

Crafts are not the only skills that can be turned into businesses. Looking after children is a skill in great demand today, and in most areas there would be no shortage of customers for a registered childminder. Computer skills too are much sought after, and many small companies will subcontract their computer work to a suitably qualified person who works from home. Often distance is no barrier. Teleworkers work for very remote employers. Companies based in North America often advertise for telework-ers anywhere in the world. Many smaller companies and publishing houses often seek the services of a copy typist – or word processor operators nowadays – to type and correct documents and manuscripts on disk.

Turn your house or land into a money earner

There are endless ways in which you can make your house or land earn you some money and these are covered in detail in Chapter 12. Almost all the options outlined in Chapter 12, ranging from running a modest bed and breakfast to running a caravan site, require a thorough knowledge of a variety of legislation and involvement in planning permission; payment of business rates; employment legislation; fire certificates; food hygiene regulations; licensing laws; and many others.

Buy an existing one-man/woman business

This can be an excellent way to start self-employment because it saves a great deal of initial research into customer demand, provided the business is healthy, the individual who is selling has a loyal client list and there is plenty of goodwill.

Often, someone who has run a successful small business as, say, a dressmaker, a mobile hairdresser or a window-cleaner has to retire, or to give up because of ill health or family commitments.

CASE HISTORY: Caroline

Caroline and her husband bought a large, very run-down Georgian house in Derbyshire because they loved it. They discovered that there was a lot of interesting history attached to the house and the surrounding land, so they set about making the house pay for itself. They took out a loan to renovate it and turned it into a corporate hospitality/conference and seminar venue. By advertising in the right business magazines and mailing suitable companies they have now built up a regular clientele of large firms that use the house and land for PR functions, training courses, survival courses and private meetings. Caroline supplies food and drink and the local hotel provides accommodation if necessary, although most of the companies use the house and land for one-day events.

CASE HISTORY: Ayesha

Ayesha intends to buy a mobile hairdressing business from a friend who is thinking of retiring. The friend has run her business for fifteen years and has built up a substantial core of regular clients. Ayesha wants a business which she can operate around her studies; she is a trained hair-dresser and has returned to college to train as an aromatherapist so that she can offer an additional service to her clients. Most of the established business's clients want their hair done in the evenings, which suits Ayesha perfectly. For the last three months she has been assisting her friend on her rounds so that the clients get to know her.

The business is thriving and provides plenty of work for one person, and the clients would be very happy for someone else to take over and continue to run the business.

You could advertise in the local paper or in shop windows that you are looking for such a business. Someone who is thinking about retiring but has not yet got around to doing anything about it may see it and act upon it. Also you can often hear of such openings through the grapevine.

The ideal scenario is that you work in tandem with that person for several months before the final takeover so that the customers get to know you and you can be sure of retaining the goodwill and the healthy customer base. Accountants working for each party can calculate the price of the business based on projected turnover, any assets (such as machinery or vehicles) and the goodwill element. From such a base you can expand if you wish when the time is right.

Buy a totally new business

'New' does not necessarily mean unproven. It is possible to buy the franchise to operate a business that has a good track record elsewhere in the country or even abroad and then develop your own customer base.

Many successful one-man/woman franchises are mobile – you take a service to the customer but you are based, for administration

---

CASE HISTORY: Aidan

Aidan was an unemployed bricklayer who was considering becoming self-employed when his father-in-law suggested that they buy a franchise. This was a mechanised repointing service for brick and stone properties, which was within both their areas of work experience. The company offered complete back-up in the form of training and marketing. Aidan and his father-in-law put some of their savings towards the cost of the franchise and got a bank loan for the rest. The bank investigated the franchise thoroughly and found it to be satisfactory.

---

purposes, at home. Examples are carpet and upholstery steam cleaning, car valeting, baked potato stands and doughnut stands. There are others which are based mainly in the home, with some travel to make deliveries, such as T-shirt or business card printing. All of these services mentioned could, of course, be set up from scratch, if your research· showed that the market demand was there. The equipment for most of these services can be bought separately and the manufacturers of the equipment will give the necessary training. Some franchises are very expensive (a minimum investment might be £3,000) and it is worth investigating whether you could assemble the whole package cheaper yourself. After all, many of the small franchises on offer are not common household names and so it is doubtful that the name itself would actually generate more sales.

Set up a new service from scratch

This is the one that requires the most market research, the most preparation and the most faith. If you are convinced that in your area, or your field of knowledge, there is a genuine need for the service you propose to offer – and it requires very little capital to start it up, thereby minimising the risk – then go for it.

There are many shining examples of how such acts of faith have paid off. Specialist mail-order services offering such products as top-quality cookware, patchwork quilt sets, hand-made wooden toys and early music cassettes, for example, have all been started by one person who believed that there was a section of the community that shared his or her interest, did some mailshots and saw things blossom from there. Many are now thriving businesses that employ dozens of people.

Sometimes it can be a glaring gap in the market and a sense of frustration that prompts someone to set up a service. The lack of a good local clock and watch repair service, fancy dress hire, children's entertainer, driving school – anything that is not easily available but you can prove that people want.

Re-inventing a product or service

This can mean taking ideas/products from the past and re-creating them for the future. Several retail and mail-order companies have successfully done this by capitalising on the modern trend of nostalgia for the past. For example, replicas of Georgian and Victorian house and garden ornaments have proved very popular. Reproductions of old nursery equipment, cookware, bed-linen and personal items have also enjoyed a revival in recent years.

It is possible to get ideas for businesses by looking at services that were provided in the past and are no longer available – a dolls' hospital, for example, where toys of all kinds are repaired. This was a commonly available service before the Second World War.

Sell goods made by other people

One example of this would be distributing foreign goods in Britain. The US Department of Trade publishes a regular magazine listing companies looking for facilities and distributors, and the British Chambers of Commerce★ has a regular listing of businesses seeking partners willing to manufacture under licence or to act as sole distributors.

On a more modest level, if selling is your forte – in other words you enjoy meeting people, talking to them, can be persuasive, have the courage to test new ground and can handle rejection – perhaps you can come to an arrangement with a friend who manufactures or produces marketable items but does not actually have the time to sell them. You could agree on a commission on each item sold and

CASE HISTORY: Paul

Paul makes pottery and has worked from home for several years. His business was in the doldrums until one day he saw a gardening programme on television which showed Victorian terracotta domes that went over rhubarb plants, or indeed any plants that needed forcing or blanching. Paul made some reproductions successfully, so he decided to try to market them. The demand was extraordinary, and he only just managed to keep up with it. He has now taken on two other potters, who both work in their own homes. He intends to copy some other pieces of antique garden pottery and market them to his existing customers.

then discuss the realistic production targets that could be met before you persuade some shop to order thousands of items that your friend cannot possibly manufacture on his or her own!

Many people make a good living out of being agents for mail-order companies – the large catalogues that offer everything for the home and family. They earn commission on each item ordered (or, rather, paid for) by the customers they get on to their books. One of the most successful international mail-order companies is Avon, the cosmetics manufacturer. They have hundreds of thousands of agents working for them all over the world.

Some children's publishers now sell to homes and schools rather than through bookshops, as the percentage of the cover price taken by the wholesalers and the retail shops is far greater than the commission paid to agents.

Other people sell successfully through 'party' schemes, selling well-known brands of clothing, jewellery, toys and even sex aids and underwear. This involves getting as many customers as possible together at a friend's house for a 'party' with wine and snacks, and persuading them to place orders for the wares. The person hosting the 'party' usually gets a payment or free gift from the salesman or woman. The aim is to hold parties in as many different areas as possible so that you tap into as many social groups as you can.

Network marketing comes under the category of selling products made by other people. The difference between being involved in network marketing and the other schemes outlined above is that most of the other sales schemes should not require the agent to part with any money at all at the outset, except perhaps in the case of the 'party' schemes where a modest sum is paid for a pack of samples, or a returnable deposit cheque is given to the manufacturers to safeguard against theft. Some network marketing schemes, on the other hand, require the participants to buy the goods or services and then sell them on. Participants also receive bonuses for recruiting other sales staff and take commissions on the new recruit's sales.

Sometimes the parent companies demand payment for providing training to the sales force. Some companies will ask for a modest registration fee (between £20 and £50) in order to eliminate time-wasters, but should provide training, whether face to face or in the form of manuals and videos, for nothing. Many people join these schemes because they are impressed by the success stories of other participants, but any company that expects you to buy a garage-full of its products and sell them on, rather than asking you to buy a few samples and then re-order when you have sold them, is not operating in a reputable way. Companies that are more concerned about the number of agents you recruit rather than the number of products you sell should be viewed with suspicion. Successful and stable companies go for slow growth of their marketing networks so that they can keep up with manufacturing

CASE HISTORY: Tricia

Tricia sells high-class costume jewellery as an agent. She usually sells through the party system, going to someone's house to demonstrate the jewellery to their friends, but sometimes she rents some space in a hospital or factory canteen and takes orders from the workers. She makes a good commission from the agency, but she does have to work at least four evenings a week and several mornings or lunch periods. She had to pay for her sample case and has to purchase any new additions to the range, but does not have to buy and resell to the customers – she just takes the orders and deducts her commission from the money she collects before processing the orders.

demand. A successful and reputable company will have regular contact with their sales agents to discuss tactics, sales opportunities and public feedback about products.

Run your own mail-order business

Mail order is one of the most popular businesses to run from home. As a form of selling it is attractive to people who have no aptitude or desire to sell face-to-face or to those who are tied to the home through disability or small children. Those who run a mail-order operation also find that they can make more profit on items if they do not sell them through shops.

A mail-order enterprise does not have to be about selling your own manufactured products. It can be a collection of other people's products that, together, represent a new idea. For example, a woman in Yorkshire found it impossible to get pure cotton clothing for her children, who both suffered badly from eczema. So she put together a collection of basic cotton clothes for babies, toddlers and children, some of which came from overseas manufacturers and marketed them through the Eczema Society and direct mail shots to doctors' surgeries and health centres.

Marketing is another important area of successful mail order. Research your market thoroughly beforehand to ensure there will be a demand for your product. Many people start off with just one product or service. They advertise this in the relevant publications and start slowly. It is important that customers are protected from unscrupulous or incompetent mail-order operations but it is equally important that any mail-order operation does not run into financial trouble early on because of extending credit to customers. Most small mail-order companies ask for payment with the order - only if you were running a business-to-business mail order set up, where you might, for example, be able to offer reputable company clients an account, would you ever get into the realms of invoicing for payment after delivery of goods. (See Chapter 8 for details of Mail Order Protection Schemes and relevant legislation for mail order operations.)

What is it that will actually earn you money?

Is it your **skill?** Do you know whether your skill is in demand, whether it has scarcity value, or whether it represents a luxury purchase or a need in today's society? Think of a skill that is in demand – invisible mending, perhaps. Commuters damage expensive suits travelling to and from the big city and they need to be repaired. Every dry cleaner offers invisible mending and this is usually done by homeworkers. All you have to do is offer your services to every dry cleaning shop in your area. If they do not need you now, they may keep your details on file for later.

Think of a skill that is rare. There is lack of watch and clock repairers in towns today, for example. Obviously, jewellers employ such craftsmen but, again, they are usually homeworkers. You could offer them your services, but you may think that there are enough people around with watch and clock problems to make it worth your while to advertise locally.

Perhaps you are a management consultant, highly skilled at assessing a company's problems and coming up with the appropriate solutions. But does the current economic climate affect your value? Are you, as a management consultant, a need, or have you become a luxury that no one can afford until times get better?

Perhaps what you are really selling is your **time?** Your skills may be limited, and your most valuable asset is that you can serve those busy customers who do not have the time to perform certain tasks themselves, such as ironing, lawnmowing, window-cleaning, dog-walking, housework, laundry, cooking, preparation for a party, typing, envelope stuffing, mailshots, and so on. When you think about ways in which you can save other people time, the list is quite long.

Then, again, perhaps it is your **effort** that is most valuable? You can do all the heavy or unpleasant jobs that your customers cannot manage – digging, building and repairs, tree-felling, cleaning stonework, laying patios, cleaning out drains, pest control, roof and gutter repair, chimney sweeping and so on. If you are strong, don't mind heights or smells, are not afraid of rats or getting yourself dirty and sweaty, then you could be in great demand!

Perhaps your **ingenuity, analytical skills and creative flair** are valuable to your customers. They come to you when they want

CASE HISTORY: Esther

Esther lives in a rural community within commuting distance of a large metropolitan area. Her children have grown up and left home and she has recently been widowed. She has no need to work from a financial point of view, but she has a need to get out of the house. Her greatest pleasure is walking her two dogs, whatever the weather. She noticed, to her distress, that many of the people in her village kept dogs but were out at work all day, leaving the dogs shut indoors for long periods. Esther decided to start up a dog-walking service. She had some leaflets printed and put them through every door in her village and the two neighbouring ones, offering to walk dogs twice a day for half an hour for a fairly modest sum. The response was tremendous. Because she is well known in the area, people are happy to give her their door keys. She lets herself in, takes the dog out for a walk and then takes it back home again. She makes a fair amount of money because she walks several dogs at once, piling them all in the back of her estate car and taking them to the nearest open area.

a problem solved, a new image, a new direction. You may be a consultant, a graphic artist, an advertising agent or a PR genius, an interior designer, a garden designer, a clothes designer or a milliner.

Or is it your **specialist knowledge** which will really earn you the money? Others benefit from your knowledge in certain areas because you do research for them, you give them health and beauty therapy or you advise them on insurance and pension plans. Perhaps you drive a taxi or are a local tourist guide – both professions requiring intimate knowledge of the local area. You can write books and articles, give lectures and demonstrations on your specialist subject. You pass your knowledge on to other people and they pay for your services.

You may have **qualifications** which equip you to train others. You are a private tutor in your own home to schoolchildren who need extra tuition in certain subjects; you perhaps teach the piano or some other musical instrument; or you train people to drive cars or ride bikes safely. Perhaps you are involved in a literacy programme or you teach English to foreigners or you are fluent in another language. Cookery and needlework can be taught in the home, as can carpentry, silver- and goldsmithing and many other crafts.

Maybe it's your **personality** that earns you money. It enables you to sell effectively, to keep small children amused, to look after the sick and the elderly, or to soothe people's troubles away with a massage and an attentive manner. You may have the skills and qualifications to be an excellent hairdresser or chiropodist but very few customers will invite you into their homes if you do not have a warm personality. It's just as important as any diploma.

Plenty of choice

We have established that there is plenty of choice for those seeking a home-based occupation – perhaps even too much. Take time to decide exactly what is right for you. It is best not to rush into anything.

If you are starting with a clean slate you need to do as much research as possible. Talk to people, listen to conversations, read the local newspapers and magazines, browse the notices in your local library, shop windows, leisure centre and parish magazine. Keep a file of information, articles and comments which will go towards pointing you in the direction of your new career.

If you want to work for someone else, get as much advice as possible about what work is available, how to apply for it and how to safeguard your rights.

Those who already know how they are going to earn money at home now need to start organising the business side of things and gathering information for the future.

Chapter 3

Working for someone else at home

In 1994 *Home Truths*, a national survey of homeworkers conducted by Ursula Huws, constructed a profile of a typical homeworker. She was a married woman in her thirties with children who worked 36 hours a week (8 of those at the weekends) and for this she earned the princely sum of £46 per week. She was most likely to do sewing work and to suffer from neck or backache or fatigue as a result of her job.

The results of *Home Truths* were shocking but they were an accurate indication of the high price some homeworkers paid for combining work and childcare under the same roof. The survey also highlighted the low pay and poor health and safety conditions under which most homeworkers laboured.

Types of work available

An audit of homeworking projects conducted by the National Group on Homeworking★ (spring 1994) showed that the clothing industry is by far the largest employer of homeworkers, or outworkers as they are often called. However, *The A to Z of Homeworking*, a list compiled by the Yorkshire and Humberside Low Pay Unit, shows a huge array of things that are assembled, packaged, processed or undertaken, mainly by women, in that region alone (see Chart on pages 46–47).

Looking for work

You may be fortunate enough to be one of those people who have been offered by your employer the opportunity to do the same job at home. This is the case with many teleworkers and a number of former factory workers doing simple assembly jobs. If you are extremely lucky you will be able to have the same benefits – employee status, pension scheme, paid holidays, paid sickness time and so on. If this is so, you will be in a very small minority.

However, if you are looking for work to do from home but are unsure what you could do, your first port of call could be your local library. A good reference library should stock various business directories which will give details about companies and what they manufacture. Some research should pinpoint those companies who assemble small items and, possibly, use homeworkers. You could then approach these companies by telephone, mail or by personal visit to see whether they do employ homeworkers and whether they have any vacancies. If they do employ homeworkers but have no vacancies, leave your details and check back with them every month or so.

Be careful

Most of the LPUs and Homeworking Projects have spent the last few years working in tandem with local Trading Standards Departments to protect people against misleading homeworking adverts and schemes.

All the LPU and Homeworking groups contacted during the writing of this book had produced an information leaflet or pack for the general public, warning against these schemes and giving advice on how to avoid becoming one of the victims of these pernicious operations. Trading Standards Departments at your local council offices should also have advice packs available.

CASE HISTORY: Morris

Morris used to work in a factory assembling computer leads. When he retired at the age of 65, the company asked him if he would like to do the same work at home as an outworker. The rates of pay being offered were the same and Morris decided that he would do it part-time to give himself a bit of extra money. He works every morning and earns about £60 from the comfort of his living room, doing a job that he finds very easy.

A academic gowns; ambulance kit bags (sewing); aprons; Aran sweaters; artificial flowers (filling pots with sand for)

B babies' blankets (crocheting); babies' dresses; badges; ball-point pens; ball bearings; bath plugs; beer mats; belts; bicycle parts; bingo ticket books; blouson jackets; board games; bolts; book indexing; boxer shorts; brass valves; Brussels sprouts (packing); buckles; budgerigar cages; burglar alarms; buttons (upholstering)

C camera bags; canoeing jackets; canvas shoes; carpet samples; chains; chappatis; children's clothes; chips (peeling potatoes); Christmas cards and gift tags; Christmas crackers; Christmas decorations; cloth (mending and burling); cloths; collars and cuffs; combs; computer leads; copper tubes; craft sewing; curtain rails; curtains; cushion covers

D data-inputting; dog collars; draught excluders; dresses; duffel coats; dusters

E electrical leads and switches; elastic (carding); embroidery; envelope addressing; equestrian products

F Fair Isle sweaters; Father Christmas hats; felt-tip pens; firemen's trousers; firework wrappers; first-aid kits; football scarves and souvenirs; fruit machines (assembly); fur coats; furnishings

G garments; glue ticketing

H hampers (mailing leaflets); handbags; hangers; hats; hoods; hooks and eyes (carding); horse blankets; hospital gowns

I induction hoops for hearing aids; insurance claims; ironing

Confidence tricks

The National Group on Homeworking and its colleague groups have become aware of three main kinds of fraudulent homeworking operations. However, there are many others, so beware.

The Directory scam Adverts are placed in the local press and shop windows asking people to send a fee (usually between £10 and £20) in return for a list of companies which offer work to homeworkers. (Most LPUs and Homeworking groups claim there is no such list, and never has been.) If the people who send off the fee

J   jackets; jewellery

K   knitting (hand and machine)

L   labels; lampshades; leaflets; leather bags, coats and jackets; leggings; light sockets; linings; lobster pots

M   maggot bags; make-up cases; manuscripts (reading); medical coats; medical supplies (packing); mice (decorative); mohair sweaters; mountaineering chalk bags

N   nails and screws; nappies; nurses' uniforms

O   onions (peeling); overalls (altering)

P   party masks; pencil sharpeners; pet products; pillowcases; plugs; pockets; popsocks; pottery cottages (painting); printed circuit boards; printed material (collating); puppets

Q   quilting cot covers and jackets; quilts (embroidering)

R   rag dolls; rag-picking; rag rugs; rattles; remote-control switches; rosettes; Rottweilers (toy); rugby shorts

S   sample books (wool, curtain fabric); scourers; shellsuits; shirts; shoeshine kits; skirts; slippers; smocking; soft toys; soldering wires and circuit boards; sponges; stickers; straws; studs for football boots

T   tea towels; telesales; tennis racquets; ties; tights; toy soldiers; tropical fish accessories; trousers; typing

U   umbrellas (inserting spokes); underwear (thermal)

V   velvet hearts; Venetian blinds; Victorian bows

W   washers; wires (crimping); word processing

Z   zips (sewing in garments)

receive a list (in many cases they never get a reply) the list will be some photocopied names and addresses of companies, each asking for registration fees of anything between £10 and £200.

The Recruitment scam   Advertisements for recruitment are placed in shop windows. You are offered money to recruit others. Having paid a fee, usually of around £15, you are then asked to place more advertisements in shop windows. For each person you recruit who sends the company £15, you only get 30p. In other words, the only way to recoup your £15 is to 'recruit' 50 other unfortunates.

The Kit scam Again, this kind of fraud is generated from adverts in the local press or even in craft magazines. Readers are invited to send money to a company in return for a kit, which can cost anything between £10 and £200. Examples of such kits include: cutting stencils out, assembling a soft toy, sewing a mock-leather wallet, making a lampshade, sewing a leather dog collar and so on. The literature claims that when you have made the product to the company's satisfaction, your initial kit fee will be refunded.

How to protect yourself

Never send money You should not have to pay a fee to secure work. A legitimate company charging a registration fee should deduct it from your first commission/sales/wages, not ask for the money up front. A genuine network marketing scheme should only ask you to pay for a small set of samples and then only after a fair amount of personal contact with the company and some training.

Read the literature carefully Does the offer seem too good to be true? Is the company offering suspiciously high rates of pay? For example, mail-order companies can address and fill their own envelopes for less than 3p per envelope so why would anyone offer to pay 50p? Is the quantity/type of work/level of skill required realistic? You may not know because you may have never tried to cut a stencil or engrave a metal disc before, but undoubtedly you would find that the task is so difficult that you would never be able to earn enough money in a week to make it worthwhile.

Beware of companies that do not give a full address or a telephone number You should be able to visit the company and speak to someone face to face; if necessary even be shown the product that you would be assembling at home. If you turn up at an address and it is an accommodation address (an office that earns money by taking in mail for people who do not have proper offices), it may be a dubious enterprise. However, the company may only have distributed their mailshot at the other end of the country, so the chances of people being able to visit are negligible. If a telephone number is given and you call it you have no way of knowing if the person who answers is in a bona fide office. One check you can make is to phone directory enquiries, give them the number and find out in what area the 'company' is supposed to be located. Then call the Trading Standards Department in that area and ask them if they have heard of the company or know of a scam being operated.

Find out more   If the company seems reputable, ask for written details, no obligation, of what work is involved, payment terms, procedures of delivery and collection of work, company liability for tax, NI, equipment etc. If the company is reluctant to do this, you have to ask yourself why.

You could ask the company if you could speak to some of their other homeworkers   A serious and committed company should offer this sort of contact anyway. The good companies use their experienced homeworkers to train up new ones or at least to provide guidance and advice during the learning process.

Looking for genuine work

Local or national firms

Contact local companies to see if they have any homeworking opportunities. If you have any previous relevant work experience, tell them about it, and also whether you have any equipment of your own at home, for example a sewing or knitting machine, and what hours you may be able to work. Also tell them about any out-side interests that you have; running social groups and serving on committees can demonstrate organisational and managerial skills as much as any work experience. Even if you know that the company does not employ homeworkers at present you may be lucky enough to catch them at the moment they are considering doing so or else inspire them to do it.

Other routes

You can ask your local trade unions if they know of any opportu-nities, but they may warn against it. The local JobCentre may have some homeworking on its books. Your local Business Link,★ Chamber of Commerce,★ or other trade organisations may have details of companies that have just started up and are employing homeworkers or who are expanding and may be doing the same. It is worth making enquiries in all sorts of places – you just never know whether you could suddenly stumble across a useful contact who can offer you a job.

Please note that the LPUs and Homeworking Groups are *not* able to tell you where you can find a job, they are primarily there to offer advice on employment rights and to undertake work that protects homeworkers from exploitation of any kind. However, they can send you advice packs which point you in the right direction when you start to look for homework.

Disabled workers

People with disabilities can contact The Royal Association for Disability and Rehabilitation (RADAR)★, the Disability Alliance★ or the Guild of Disabled Homeworkers★ for specialist advice. (RADAR's booklets *Into Work – a guide for disabled people* and *Self Employment – A Positive Option* are particularly helpful.) Your local JobCentre may also be able to help. Every JobCentre should have a Disability Employment Adviser (DEA). He or she may cover several JobCentres over the course of a week and if you are unable to go to the JobCentre, the DEA will visit your home. A DEA will help you plan a strategy for getting back to work, in the form of a Back To Work plan. He or she may call in a Placement, Assessment and Counselling Team (PACT) first. There are around 60 PACTs in the UK, operating out of local JobCentres, and their job is to provide an advice and assessment service for employers and disabled.

CASE HISTORY: Barbara

Barbara is disabled and a young mother. She wanted to get some work at home and contacted one of the organisations for the disabled, which put her in touch with several companies. Eventually she found a home job which was not too demanding – inspecting nylon stockings prior to packing. The company delivers to Barbara several hundred stockings in boxes, having supplied her with a flesh tone 'leg' on a stand. Wearing cotton gloves, she has to pull each nylon stocking over the leg and check that it is not flawed or snagged. The company is a fair employer and gives its workers employees status and pension rights, if they qualify. They have a homework organiser who regularly visits all the workers and keeps them in touch with each other. Although Barbara does not earn very much, she likes the work and the company.

Teleworkers

Teleworkers are those people who work using information and communications technologies from their own homes, or from a nearby business centre, telecentre or telecottage where multimedia technology is available for individuals to buy time on. Teleworkers can either work for themselves or for an employer. Since the early 1990s many large companies have decentralised by offering their data processors and other computer personnel the chance to work from home whilst linked up to the head office by email, fax and phone. It is not unusual for teleworkers to find jobs with companies that can be over 3,000 miles away. Location is no longer important.

The first stop in the search for a job is to join the Telework, Telecottage and Telecentre Association (TCA)* and get a copy of their very useful *Teleworking Handbook*. Specialist magazines such as *Teleworker*, published by the TCA, carry adverts for jobs.

The Internet is becoming a very useful source of information on teleworking and available jobs. Members of the TCA who subscribe to the TCA Online Service get details of information about work emailed to them. At the time of writing, a web site called TeleMart, an EU-sponsored teleworker marketing project, offers opportunities for freelance teleworkers to register with brokers. There are also several teleworker employment agencies on the Internet. If you are in full-time employment at the moment and your company is thinking about starting a teleworking scheme, you should think about your rights as an employee before volunteering.

The white collar union MSF offers the following advice:

- Teleworking should always be voluntary. Make sure you retain the right to return to office-based working if you find that you cannot cope with the isolation. Ask for an annual or bi-annual review of your job situation.
- You should expect to remain an employee of the company with full employee's rights and not become a self-employed subcontractor.
- You should have the same benefits, rates of pay, leave periods, pensions and training and promotion opportunities as office-based employees – except, of course, if you no longer have to travel around for the company, it would be unreasonable to expect a company car, for example.

- It is suggested that your contract of employment requires regular meetings with other colleagues and managers, to lessen your sense of isolation. (Of course, you may prefer it that way. Becoming a teleworker has given you that long-desired opportunity to move to the Shetland Isles!)
- Your employers should pay for or provide all the equipment, telephone line/ISDN line, if appropriate. Maintenance arrangements and any additional costs incurred in setting aside a room for teleworking such as heating, lighting and insurance should also be the responsibility of the employer. You could even ask your employer to pay a rental for use of the room.
- Your employer should accept liability for any accident or injury which occurs while teleworking at home. Health and safety requirements mean that the employer should assess the home workplace (for electrical power supply, safety of equipment and ergonomic use of equipment, for example).

Never waste an opportunity

Ask friends and neighbours if they know of anything, particularly if you are a mother with children – some of the best homeworking

---

CASE HISTORY: Rani

Rani started her working life as a teleworker when her employer, a major national bank, decided to offer some of its computer staff the chance to work from home, processing data. She jumped at the opportunity. Her salary was very slightly reduced but she was provided with all the necessary hardware to enable her to work from home. However, after a while the bank became involved in a merger and decided to abandon the experiment of using teleworkers. Although Rani was offered her old job back at the head office in London, she had become used to not commuting and wanted to stay at home. She joined the TCA and answered an advertisement in its magazine for a bank in America who wanted someone to process cheque payments in sterling in the UK. Rani got the job. She now receives a weekly download of data from the USA, which she processes, printing out cheques, orders and statements, which are then collected by bike for the manager of the London branch to check and sign.

---

jobs can come from knowing someone at mother and toddler or playgroup who has a good homeworking job. Leads on jobs can come from the most surprising quarters. It is always worth mentioning that you would like to work from home when you go to parties or other functions. You might just be sitting next to a businessman or woman who is thinking of farming out some work to homeworkers.

When you find work

You need to ask yourself, and the company offering the work, the following questions before accepting:

What is expected of you?

Have you done this type of work before? If not, can you cope with it? Is any training given? Does it involve assembling materials and do you have the room at home to spread the work out? Can you meet the delivery dates? Is it close work and is your eyesight up to it? What quality of work will you be expected to deliver and how will that quality be measured? If your work is continually substandard, will someone help you to achieve the necessary standard?

Is there a minimum quantity required?

Find out how much work you have to do to make a living wage or how many pieces have to be completed each week for the company to continue giving you work. It may be the case that if you cannot complete a minimum requirement of, say, 1,000 cards of hooks and eyes a week, they will give the work to someone else. Companies cannot afford to have stock tied up with workers who cannot meet their quotas.

Is there a co-ordinator or group leader to turn to for advice?

It is not enough to have contact once a week or less with the person who delivers your work, or from whom you pick it up. You need to have access over the telephone to someone who can answer your day-to-day queries.

Is there a manual to help you?

You need a manual that explains your equipment so that you can diagnose any faults or cope with any problems. Some companies, particularly in the clothing industry, have specification manuals because they are producing items of clothing for big chain stores who are very strict in their requirements. These manuals will explain the exact size of buttonholes required, how the buttons are to be sewn on a shirt and so on.

What quantity of material will be delivered each week?

Can you store it? Twelve thousand buttons to be carded may not take up much room but 12 dozen teddy bears that need eyes sewn on will. Be realistic about your storage capacity.

Is the company properly insured?

The company should be fully insured for loss, theft and fire risk while the goods are in your home. This should not be your responsibility. They should also be insured for goods in transit, even if you are fetching and carrying the goods yourself. If the company does not insure them, maybe you should look elsewhere for work.

Does your tenancy/mortgage/insurance allow this sort of work?

If you are a council tenant you should be aware that certain local authorities require homeworkers to have written permission from them to do work at home. Most tenancy agreements prohibit the use or storage in the home of any inflammable materials, liquids, gases or chemicals, other than those normally required for household jobs. Consequently, you must be wary of any homework which requires you to glue, paint or spray. If any fire broke out in your home and such materials were found to be present it would undoubtedly invalidate your contents and building insurance.

Will your neighbours object?

Council tenants are usually prohibited in their lease from undertaking any activity which might cause a nuisance or inconvenience to neighbours. Neighbours may object to your receiving frequent deliveries by lorry of materials. They may also object to any noise caused by machinery: some industrial sewing machines can be very noisy. The West Yorkshire Homeworking Group recommends the following:

- moving the machine away from a shared wall and from a hollow floor to a solid floor
- using a heavy rubber mat (or pieces of carpet underlay) under the machine to reduce vibration
- having your machine serviced
- changing to a quieter machine – some employers may swap the machine if you point out that complaints about noise from neighbours might mean you have to stop doing the homework.

How will you be paid?

Will you be paid cash in hand, by cheque or by direct debit? Weekly, monthly or at the end of a period of seasonal work? You need to know from the start. You also need to check who will be paying tax and National Insurance – you or the company providing you with work.

Is the work seasonal?

Certain work is obviously seasonal – making Christmas decorations, packing Christmas cards or filling Christmas crackers, for example – but there can also be seasonal highs and lows in other industries. Some firms may only take on outworkers to meet the demand of the pre-season period.

Can the company offer you other work?

Ask if the company can offer you work all year round, even if it is of a different nature. If not, try to get a precise idea of when the seasonal work will start and stop so that you can look for other work to fill in the gaps.

Can you visit the factory?

A company with nothing to hide should be pleased to allow factory visits. You can then see the processes which lead up to your work. It should also give you an opportunity to talk to some full-time workers and gauge whether the company is an employer with a good track record.

Does the type of work allow you to be flexible?

If you have children and you need to work around them, you need work that can be done at any time of the day, as long as you are able to fill your quota for the week. Some jobs will not offer that flexibility. You may be doing typing or invoicing at home and receiving daily deliveries or fax transmissions of material that needs to be done immediately. You cannot cope with that if you have to attend to your children as well. Make sure you fully understand the time schedule of any work that is on offer before you take it on.

Does the employer/company provide you with equipment?

There are various scenarios here.

- You are provided with the necessary equipment and servicing back-up. This is the ideal situation to be in.
- You are provided with the equipment and asked to pay a deposit against it, which is refunded after a trial period. This is not ideal but understandable from the employer's point of view, particularly if you are a new outworker. For all they know you could disappear tomorrow, taking the equipment with you.
- You are asked to buy the equipment by having a small amount deducted from your wages each week. This is only suitable if the company wishes you to be self-employed and agrees that you can then use that equipment to do work for other companies – in the case of computer equipment, for example, or an industrial sewing machine. Check that the price they are asking for their equipment is comparable to that of equipment available on the open market.
- You are expected to provide your own equipment. In the case of small items, such as tools, paintbrushes, hand-sewing or knitting equipment, this is fair enough, but do not agree to buy major items outright.

CASE HISTORY: Priya

Priya found work machining canvas bags for a sports and leisure wear company which employs outworkers all over the north of England. The company supplied Priya with her machine but she pays a weekly rental for the use of it. A company employee came to her home and spent a couple of hours showing her how to operate the machine and put the bags together. She has a telephone number she can ring if she has any problems. The canvas parts are delivered on Monday mornings and the completed bags are collected on Thursdays. Priya is paid by the piece and earns roughly £2 an hour, which is quite good compared with the hourly rate that some of her friends get. She manages to amass about £50 a week but it is very hard work: six hours' machining a day makes her shoulders and neck ache.

Do you have to buy anything else from the company?

Some sales schemes expect participants to buy a case of samples. This is common practice and a reasonable safeguard against losing thousands of pounds' worth of valuable stock.

Can you plan ahead?

You need to know whether or not you can take holidays or take a break for personal reasons, or pack up work for the children's school holidays without losing your chance to work for that company again. Check the position before you start work.

Health and safety

You must not undertake any work which would be prejudicial to your own health and safety and, as you are working from home, that of your family.

Some Homeworking Groups report that employers have given their homeworkers chemicals and glues in unmarked tins and jars. This is against the law. The company should inform you exactly what substances you will be working with, how to handle them and what action to take to avoid illness or injury. For example, fumes from solvents and glues can be very dangerous, even lethal. They can cause headaches, dizziness, various allergies and heart and lung disease. Some are even known to be carcinogenic.

Similarly, working with fibres – cloth, furs, wool – can cause health problems such as skin rashes, allergies and sore throats. The dust created when machine knitting wool passes at speed through the circles of wax into the needles can cause breathing problems for sensitive people.

Continual hunching over a sewing machine can cause back, shoulder, neck and eye problems, while long hours in front of a VDU screen can cause eye strain, headaches, dizziness, nausea and muscle fatigue. Your local Environmental Health Department or relevant trade union will be able to supply you with information on how to avoid a range of work-related accidents or health problems, from asthma to repetitive strain injury (RSI).

Take sensible precautions

Good lighting, ventilation and seating, as well as frequent rest breaks, are very important for all types of repetitive work. Machinery and electrical equipment must have safety guards to minimise the risk of accident. You should confirm that your power supply is correctly protected and adequate for the task; also, that the company providing the machine has checked that it is both mechanically and electrically safe to use.

It cannot be stressed too often that you need a separate, prefer-ably lockable room in which to do your work, particularly if you have children in the house. If possible, keep all flammable materials locked up outside the house, or in a lockable metal filing cabinet, and keep only the minimum necessary for immediate use. Never smoke when dealing with flammable materials. Do not have your work room next to the children's bedrooms; in any case, ensure that the work room is properly ventilated to avoid and evacuate concen-trations of fumes and dust. Do not store any flammable materials in a room that gets very warm, such as a loft in summer, or near a source of heat, such as a radiator. Keep plastic packaging materials away from small children and babies. If you are dealing with mate-rials that increase the risk of fire, seek advice from the Fire

---

CASE HISTORY: Sean

Sean was made redundant and was unable to get another job for a variety of reasons. Finally, the local JobCentre offered him some outwork, stuffing envelopes for a mail order company. Although the work is boring and repetitive, it is very easy and he can fit it in whenever he feels like it. Sometimes his wife helps him in the evenings and he has found that he can earn about £80 in a good week.

Prevention Officer at your local fire station on measures you can take to keep you and your family safe.

If you are engaged in sewing work, check that you are not scattering needles or pins around the house that could injure people or pets.

If you are worried about the physical side-effects that your work may be having on you or your family, discuss it with your provider of work. If you get no help there, contact one of the relevant organisations listed at the back of this book, your local Environmental Health Department or a local trade union.

The National Group on Homeworking gives the following health and safety tips for working at home:

Substances and materials

If your work involves using substances and chemicals, e.g. solvents or paints, they should be clearly labelled. The company for whom you are doing the work must supply you with information about the substances and chemicals you are working with, such as:

- Are they flammable or toxic?
- Do they give off fumes? (Is the room where you work well ventilated? Can you open the windows?)
- How should they be stored?
- Do you need protective clothing, e.g. gloves or masks?
- Does the work produce a lot of mess or waste materials?
- If so, is the waste a fire hazard? (The company who supplies you with work should collect it regularly.)

Equipment and tools

- Does your work require certain equipment and tools to do the job properly?
- Does the equipment need to be regularly serviced and maintained?
- Does the work involve a lot of close up detailed work? Do you need extra lighting?
- Do you need protective equipment, e.g. a machine guard?
- Do you ever suffer from neck/backache or general aches and muscle fatigue? You may need an adjustable chair with good back support or an adjustable but stable desk to do your work. You may also need a footrest.
- Does the equipment need a power supply? If so, is it safe? You may need a circuit breaker.

Working Time regulations

The Working Time regulations came into effect on 10 October 1998. One of the most important provisions is that guaranteeing employees who have completed over three months' continuous service, three weeks' paid holiday a year, rising to four weeks in November 1999. Other provisions relate to the average hours of work, night-shifts and daily and weekly rest periods. Employers are under a duty to keep suitable records.

National Minimum Wage

A large variety of work is available to homeworkers – far more than is listed here – but, at the moment, the work is often irregular and low-paid. However, the National Minimum Wage Act is due to come into force in April 1999, which will impose a minimum wage of between £3.00 and £3.60 an hour depending upon status. It has been agreed by the government that workers aged between 18 and 21 years can be paid a development rate of £3.00 per hour. Workers aged 22 years or above who are beginning a new job and receiving accredited training, leading to a recognised qualification, can be paid a development rate of £3.20 per hour for the first six months. Thereafter, the rate should be the full £3.60 per hour.

How will this affect homeworkers?

Many companies using homeworkers prefer them to be self-employed because it is cheaper (no overheads) and they do not have as much responsibility for self-employed workers as they would for employees. The NMW Act expressly applies to all workers as defined by the Act and to homeworkers who do not otherwise fall under this category. Even if the homeworkers are self-employed, generally speaking they will for the most part be deemed to be workers and will benefit from protection under the Act.

The NMW Act requires all employers to keep records of pay and hours worked. Workers will be able to require their employer to produce these records for inspection and take copies of them. The Low Pay Units (LPUs) are still advising all homeworkers to also keep their own strict records of hours worked, whether the work is regular, whether you have any sort of contract or agreement, what you are paid and whether any deductions are made. This information may be useful at a later date if there is some dispute about status and any entitlement to National Minimum Wage. If an employer fails to produce the relevant records, a worker will have the right to take action through an employment tribunal and any records that worker has kept will be very valuable. Under the new law, employers can be heavily penalised for failing to be fair. For example, just failing to produce employment records at the worker's request can result in a tribunal making the employer pay the worker in question 80 times the hourly NMW as compensation.

Even if you are genuinely self-employed – you may proof-read for several publishing houses, or do assembly work for several manufacturers – you should expect to get at least NMW rates.

There will be some difficulty in applying the NMW to piece workers (workers who get paid per number of units or pieces that they complete, rather than by the hour). At the time of writing, no solution to this dilemma had been published, but the Low Pay Commission (the body established to investigate low pay problems) has recommended that employers use a 'pay reference period' system, whereby piece work and work that has seasonal fluctuations can be worked out to produce an average output per hour and thus a reasonable rate of pay. The pay reference period over which the output can be averaged may not exceed the period of one month.

Employers will also have to provide each homeworker with a detailed statement to enable each worker to ensure that they are being paid the NMW. Any worker being paid less than the NMW will be able to recover the difference through a tribunal or county court.

It is hoped that the NMW Act will prove to be workable, although most of the LPUs and Homeworking Groups are preparing to face a couple of years of doing battle with those companies that persistently try to flout the law.

What are your rights?

If you are a full-time employee you are entitled to:

- an itemised payslip, whether you receive your wages by cash, cheque or direct debit. This payslip should show gross wages and any deductions for tax, National Insurance, pension scheme, etc., and final net pay
- a contract of employment, stating the terms and conditions under which you are employed. This should be given to you within 13 weeks of your starting employment. It should detail pay, sick pay, holiday entitlements (if any), hours to be worked (perhaps a minimum or a maximum), the dates when work is due to start and finish, the scale and rate of pay for piece work, and how often monies are to be paid
- irrespective of length of service or hours of work, all women are entitled to 14 weeks' maternity leave and the right to return to the same, or similar, job. Women with two years' service before the eleventh week before the expected week of confinement (EWC) have the right to 29 weeks' maternity leave.
- maternity pay is payable to women who have been employed continuously in the same job for 26 weeks before the 15th week before the EWC and they have average weekly earnings of at least the lower earnings limit (£64 in 1998). Maternity pay is 90 per cent of average earnings for six weeks, followed by 12 weeks at £57.70 per week. Women who earn below the lower earnings limit but who have paid Class 1 NI contributions for at least 26 weeks out of the previous 66 will receive an allowance of £57.70 for the statutory number of weeks.

- Statutory Sick Pay (SSP) If you have worked for the same employer continuously for three months and have made adequate National Insurance contributions, you are eligible for SSP. You are not paid for the first three days of absence. In 1998/9 the maximum weekly amount of SSP is £57.50.
- redundancy payment if you have worked for the same employer from the age of 18 for more than two years
- compensation for unfair dismissal, provided you can prove your claim, if you have worked for the same employer for more than two years
- a period of notice, if you have worked for an employer for over one month
- join a trade union if you wish, without being penalised by your employer
- equal pay, regardless of your sex or race, whether you work from home or in the factory.

National Insurance and tax

If you are self-employed, read Chapter 6, which deals fully with the subjects of National Insurance (NI) and tax.

If you are an employee, NI and tax should be deducted from your wages by your employer if you earn over a certain amount each week (currently £64). If you earn less than that you are exempt from NI.

The amount of income you are allowed to earn before paying tax (tax year 1998/9) is as follows:

Basic personal allowance for everyone under the age of 65	£4,195
Persons aged 65–74	£5,410
Persons aged 75 or over	£5,600

Allowances that reduce tax

Married couple's allowance	– under 65	£285.00
	– 65–74	£495.75
	– 75 and over	£501.75

Additional personal allowance, widow's bereavement allowance, and allowance for maintenance payments each give a maximum tax reduction of £285.

Tax rates for 1998-9 are as follows:

Lower rate band	income up to £4,300	taxed at 20 per cent
Basic rate band	£4,301–£27,100	taxed at 23 per cent (normal rate) taxed at 20 per cent (savings income rate)
Higher rate band	income over £27,100	taxed at 40 per cent

Personal reliefs for 1998/9 are as follows:

Mortgage interest, borrowings up to £30,000	tax relief restricted to 10 per cent
Enterprise Investment Scheme up to £150,000	tax relief restricted to 20 per cent
Venture Capital Trust up to £100,000	tax relief restricted to 20 per cent

Rent-a-Room exempt on gross annual rent of up to £4,250 per annum. (See Chapter 12.)

Relief for the married couple's allowance and the allowances linked to it will be restricted to 10 per cent in 1999/2000 and the additional personal allowance has been extended to women with children and incapacitated husbands living with them.

Working Families Tax Credit (WFTC)
This will replace the existing Family Credit from October 1999. WFTC is payable to families where at least one of the parents works 16 hours or more a week. The rate of WFTC is based on the number of children, with an extra credit for parents working 30 hours or more per week. In addition, a childcare tax credit will be included worth 70 per cent of eligible childcare costs. Where a family's net income (excluding WFTC and child benefit) is more than £90 per week, WFTC is reduced by 55p for every £1 of net income.

Self-assessment
The 1994 Finance Act requires all taxpayers to keep records of their income and capital gains to enable them to complete a tax return. These have to be kept, usually until 22 months after the end of the tax year to which they relate.

Self-employed people and partners will have to hold on to the records of their income and capital gains for five years after the fixed filing date. You are encouraged to calculate your own tax, or, if you wish, the Inland Revenue will do it for you, free of charge. Many people, of course, who are self-employed or starting up a small business from home will have an accountant who will do this for them anyway.

Booklets explaining self-assessment in detail can be obtained from your nearest Inland Revenue office.

Taxable benefits

The following state benefits are taxable – in other words, they count towards your total income for tax purposes.

* State retirement pension
* Widow's pension
* Industrial injuries/death benefit widow's pension
* Invalid Care Allowance
* Jobseeker's Allowance (This is taxable for the first year)
* Income Support (A married man's Income Support is split into two parts for tax purposes: his part is taxable, his family's is not)
* Incapacity Benefit (see below)

All other state benefits – maternity, child, sickness, etc. – are non-taxable.

Disability benefits

With effect from 13 April 1995 Incapacity Benefit replaced Invalidity Benefit and sickness benefit. If you are in receipt of Incapacity Benefit you can earn up to £48 per week without your benefit being affected as long as you work less than 16 hours. This is called 'therapeutic earnings' and you have to get a doctor's note to say that in his or her opinion the work 'helps to improve, to prevent or delay deterioration in, the disease or bodily or mental disablement'.

Disability Living Allowance, which is payable to disabled people under the age of 65 and comes in two parts – mobility and care allowances – is completely non-taxable; you can be a millionaire and still receive this benefit.

Chapter 4

The importance of market research

If you are still in the process of choosing an occupation or business idea to pursue at home, market research is an essential part of your decision-making process. Its value cannot be underestimated. It will help you to invest wisely, and, later, it will enable you to keep ahead of the game by expanding, diversifying or contracting. Market research is so vital to most British companies that they spend over £200m a year commissioning special research by professionals.

'Market Research is the voice of the consumer. It is vital to industry, commerce and government. It is the means by which ordinary people can influence the development and marketing of goods and services and the formulation of social policy,' says the Market Research Society,* which is the incorporated professional body for those individuals who use survey techniques for market, social and economic research.

Don't fall into the trap of thinking that this has nothing to do with you: the techniques for researching potential markets can be used by everyone and, in this information age where huge amounts of data are readily available in all forms, the lone individual can easily reap the benefits of some very expensive corporate research without going further than a regional library.

Where will my customers come from?

For those who wish to be self-employed, this is the burning question. You make a product, perhaps several products, or supply a service but where will you sell this product/service?
• the general public

- specialist markets
- other businesses
- retail outlets.

Will your market be:

- local
- regional
- national
- overseas?

CASE HISTORY: Stephen

Stephen's home-made fishing flies were often admired by fellow anglers. He decided to research the market to see whether he could set up in business making these flies. He went to the library and was advised by the librarian to look at several press directories which contained details of all the fishing publications in the country and their circulations. He discovered that the combined circulations of the magazines represented a large market. He then looked through several *Yellow Pages* directories for different areas and photocopied the pages of fishing shops. He rang many of the shops at random and asked them where they bought their flies and whether they would be interested in a new source of supply.

After a lot more research into his market-place Stephen set up his business, starting by selling to shops. Eventually he progressed to mail order.

Making the decision at which market sector to aim your product/service is inextricably linked to how, eventually, you will market it – that is to say, how you will reach the market you have targeted. You may say, 'Well, I thought I would sell to the local general public by just putting an ad in the local newspaper.' That may work if you are a jobbing gardener or a hairdresser but, even then, you might get work faster if you found out which people were most likely to want your product/service and addressed your sales pitch directly to them.

Sources of information

Libraries

The best libraries in which to start your search are either good reference libraries or what are known as business libraries, which are usually found in large towns or regional centres. These are ordinary libraries but the reference section specialises in information, in many forms, about commerce and industry and related matters. The librarians are trained to help you wade productively through the available information or, if they have not got it, to tell you what you need and where to get it. Hospitals, colleges and universities also have libraries that may hold the relevant information you require.

You may be saying, 'I just make patchwork bags; how is a visit to the library going to help me?' If all you have been doing is taking your wares, week after week, to craft fairs and hoping to sell one or two, a visit to an appropriate library could help you find a better, bigger and more reliable market for your goods.

CASE HISTORY: Tom

Tom invented a gadget which stored computer disks safely but he did not know whether it was marketable and whether he should go to the expense of taking out a patent. He went to a large business library and spent a whole week reading all the past year's reports and surveys on computer equipment that had appeared in newspapers and business magazines. He then obtained lists of manufacturers of computer accessories from a manufacturers' directory and rang them to ask if they manufactured something similar to his invention. None of them did and many of them were very interested. He went ahead and applied for a patent, then sold the rights to manufacture to a Scottish company.

Directories

Good reference libraries stock all kinds of directories. You can find out, for example, the titles of all the craft/needlework magazines published in the UK by consulting, for example, *Benn's Media* or *BRAD*. You may then consider advertising in some or all of these, thereby reaching a specialist audience that would be interested in your products. A reference library should have all the *Yellow Pages* directories for the UK. You could photocopy the pages which contain the gift/craft shops and send them all a mailshot (selling your products on a regular basis through shops would give you some security). Most reference libraries stock the *Directory of British Associations* which gives details of associations, societies, institutes, regional and local organisations, chambers of commerce and national federations. Say, for example, you decided that your product would appeal to the members of women's organisations. The *Directory* would give you the addresses of the national body of the Women's Institute, Townswomen's Guild, Mothers' Union and so on. You could then write to them to buy advertising in their magazines or pay to insert leaflets in their mailshots.

So, just a couple of hours' research can open up some positive markets for the woman who makes patchwork bags. It is also worth pointing out that by exploring these markets you may find out that the product/service you are offering is not as marketable as you thought and this will influence you to adapt or abandon your scheme.

CASE HISTORY: Gloria

Gloria wrote and published her own book about jam-making, but not before she had thoroughly researched the market for her book. When it was still in the manuscript stage, she went through the *Directory of British Associations* and noted down all the women's groups in the country that would have an interest in domestic arts. She had a book jacket designed and used it as the basis of a leaflet and order form which she mailed to the secretaries of all the women's groups for them to distribute. Once the orders started coming in, she risked getting the book published by a local printer who specialised in 'short runs'. The price of her book had been very carefully worked out before she advertised. The book was a modest success and she now plans another cookery book using the same marketing route.

If you have no experience of doing research you can go up to the librarian (try to pick a quiet period) armed with a list of questions.

For example, you may be considering setting up a sandwich delivery service for local industries, so you ask, 'How do I find out how many industrial estates are in the area?' (The librarian may point you towards the local authority planning department.) Or, you may be considering marketing your house as a film location and you ask, 'Is there a directory of television and film production companies?' (There is more than one. If your library does not stock them the librarian can tell you the names of the publishers if you want to buy copies, or which library in your region does stock them.) You may manufacture a product which would interest the head teachers of primary schools and you ask, 'Is there a list of primary schools for the whole country?' (The librarian will say yes; he or she may have to point you to a government source for the information, but first will arm you with the necessary information to ask for the right publication.)

And so on – the possibilities are endless. Libraries not only stock information in book form but on microfiche and often CD as well. They may stock a whole year's back issues of trade or business magazines or national newspapers. You can look through them to see whether a particular topic of interest to you and relevant to your product/service has been covered in depth. If you are fortunate, your library may also offer reader access to the Internet. Don't forget that any statistics published can be used in the marketing of your product. For example, if you run a carpet and upholstery cleaning service, it would be useful to quote in your sales literature from any relevant research published by, say, the British Carpet Manufacturers Association. You could find out about this by reading through back issues of the appropriate trade magazine.

Other professional sources

Alternative sources of information are local Chambers of Commerce,★ Enterprise Agencies, regional branches of the Department of Trade and Industry,★ and Training and Enterprise Councils (TECs).★ They can also help you with further advice, give you literature, point you in the direction of companies that sell mailing lists for particular market sectors, introduce you to people with whom you may possibly enter a productive business relationship and so on.

CASE HISTORY: Janet

Janet has a degree in textile design and wanted to work from home as a freelance. Her Local Enterprise Agency was able to provide her with lists of textile manufacturers in the UK to whom she could offer her services. The Enterprise Agency was also able to point her in the direction of information about arts and crafts grants and other financial information to help her through her first year.

If you make a product or provide a service which you feel would be successful abroad contact in the first instance your Business Link Office★ if you live in England. If you are resident in Scotland, contact Scottish Enterprise,★ in Wales contact Business Connect.★

Chambers of Commerce deserve a second mention here because they have often built up productive relationships with overseas business groups and can also provide contacts and information.

The commercial sections of embassies in the UK are a valuable source of information – for example, the US Embassy in London has a huge reference library and can offer all kinds of help.

The Internet

You have to view the Internet as the world's largest library, at your fingertips. If you do not have personal access to the Internet, then there may be a large reference library nearby that does. Some colleges and universities offer an access service for a fee. Many large towns now have cybercafés where you can get online for a small fee. You pay for the hours you use.

To access the Internet from home you need five things: a modern telephone connection with a socket, a computer, a modem (if your computer does not already have one), a subscription to an Internet service and suitable software. You will have to consider two costs: to buy your Internet access either from an Internet access provider (IAP) or an online service provider; and your telephone charges.

IAPs provide only a 'raw' connection to the Internet, while online services are more like an electronic magazine, with Internet access offered almost as an afterthought. Most online services charge a monthly membership of around £5, which gives three or four hours' access a month plus unlimited access to certain services. Most providers also offer an unlimited access monthly rate of around £15 to £20 a month, depending on the volume of services they offer in addition to basic access. They may, for example, offer you free web space of your own, where you can advertise your products or invite other web users to contact you with information, etc. *The Which? Guide to the Internet* includes very useful information on how to harness the Internet for your small business and how to choose between providers and to access the Internet cost-effectively.

Conducting your own survey

British businesses spend millions of pounds each year getting professional researchers to conduct surveys on their behalf and, as discussed in the first part of this chapter, you can reap the benefit of some of that research if it is published. You can also take a leaf out of the big companies' book and conduct a modest survey of your own. It is not difficult and it can pay surprising dividends.

It can mean pounding the streets, knocking on doors or stopping passers-by. A significant proportion of people will not co-operate, but in the end it will be worth your while, provided the questions are framed properly to give you accurate information.

First, be clear in your mind *exactly* what you want to find out. If you are searching for an occupation and have not yet decided what it should be, perhaps you need to canvass house-to-house in the area to find out what services people want? You need concise questions that prompt simple answers. For example:

1 Do you employ a gardener?   Yes/No
2 Would you like to employ a gardener?   Yes/No
3 (If the answer to question 2 is yes)   What jobs would you most want a gardener to do?   Weeding/mowing the lawn/digging/repairing the fences/taking all the garden rubbish away/designing a new garden.

From that simple questionnaire you might be able to ascertain that most people already employ a gardener – so no work there for you. Alternatively, you may discover that most people would like to employ a gardener (but have not done so far) and that the job they most want done is mowing the lawn.

Your next piece of market research is to find out what the competition is charging by telephoning a few jobbing gardeners and asking their prices. If you can undercut them and still make a living, the next step is to print some leaflets offering lawnmowing services at so much per hour and stick them through the doors of the people you have surveyed.

Surveys don't have to be conducted door-to-door, of course. They can be carried out by post but, unless you are prepared to offer stamped self-addressed envelopes, the chances are you will get very few replies. You might be able to come to an arrangement with a magazine to distribute surveys on your behalf. For example, perhaps the church magazine would, for a fee (and provided they felt the subject matter was in keeping), insert your survey in its pages and ask members to drop the completed survey into a box (which you would provide) when they next attend church. This was the route by which one entrepreneur arrived at a local pet-sitting service.

You may be considering setting up a baby-sitting service, in which case you could ask the local mother and toddler groups, playgroups and nursery schools if they would distribute your survey to the parents and, again, you would provide a box in which the completed surveys were collected.

Perhaps you are planning to offer a car-valeting service. You could approach local offices and factories which have large numbers of personnel who commute to work by car and ask if you could survey them to see whether they would be interested in having their car valeted while they work.

There are lots of 'captive' markets that could be explored in this fashion and then targeted.

Using professional routes

It is possible to buy into what are called Omnibus Surveys. These are surveys that are continuously conducted by professional market

---

CASE HISTORY: Angela

Angela had often thought that commuters from her two local stations would be interested in buying sandwiches, tea and coffee before they boarded the morning trains to London. There were no existing facilities, as the stations were fairly remote. She was offered the chance to buy a mobile shop van which would be ideal as a sandwich bar. Before she took the plunge, she conducted her own survey among all the commuters who took trains every day between 6.30a.m. and 8.30a.m. Most of the replies were positive so she contacted Railtrack, who owned the station and car park, to ask if, for a fee, she could park outside their stations in the morning. They agreed, provided she did not obstruct car parking, and her business was born.

---

research companies amongst specific markets. You can, for a relatively modest fee, buy some space on these surveys and insert some questions of your own. For example, you may be considering producing a self-help book for people with a specific medical problem. You could buy some questions on a regular survey which is sent out to GPs all over the UK. You could ask those GPs if they would find such a book valuable; whether there is a book that they recommend to patients; and how many patients they have on their register suffering from this condition. The research company would then collate the answers and present you with the results.

Some market research companies regularly produce in-depth market reports about certain industries, markets or social groups. Mintel, for example, publishes regular business and industry reports. You can buy these reports although they are usually quite expensive because of the man-hours put into the research, or access them via the Internet. Many government departments also produce regular surveys about certain social groups. If the sort of information you need is contained in any of these, then reading them can be immensely valuable.

Other ways of gathering information

Using your eyes and ears is important. You can glean lots of useful information by talking to people and learning from the mistakes of others.

Many craft workers, unfortunately, take a 'scatter gun' approach to marketing their wares, mainly by renting stalls at the many craft fairs held all over the country every week. This can often be a total waste of time and money. Try to attend as many fairs as you can before choosing the venues at which you will rent a stall. Spend a day at a fair and watch the various stalls. You will probably notice that the very beautiful and expensive items do not sell at all but the stallholders dispense leaflets and business cards in the hope that a percentage of the public who are browsing will come back to them at a later date and commission something special. This is not a cost-effective use of time. You may note that certain items always sell quickly – preserves, herbal products, cushions, small pictures of local views, for example. Take note of the price ranges and what most people are prepared to pay for items. Listen to the public as they walk out of the fair or while they are having a cup of tea, and note their comments. They may indicate preferences or discuss prices or compare one craft fair with another. Look at the locations of the stalls. Does the stall nearest to the tea stand attract the most customers, or the one nearest the door? What display equipment do the busiest stalls have? Is there a steady flow of customers through the doors? Has the weather affected the attendance? Is there enough parking for everyone? All these factors have a bearing on whether a particular craft fair is a good market-place for you to invest the time and money to display your wares.

Reading local newspapers is important. You can pick up some very useful information about perceived gaps in the market from comments in the features or from the wanted ads. Perhaps a local councillor gives an interview in which he or she says that the council has decided to give financial and practical aid to local tourism projects, in which case your plan to turn your front room into a tea shop would be a suitable project for them to consider. Perhaps a local conservation group is offering a grant for any undertaking that involves beautifying the local villages. This might just fit in with your proposed business of establishing and maintaining hanging baskets on lamp posts.

You will find sections in local newspapers that describe the activities of special interest groups in the area. These may be some of the captive markets for which you are looking. Perhaps someone may complain in an article about the lack of a certain service or facility in the area and you can think of a way of filling the gap, or you may read about the imminent closure of a business and move in to take over its customers.

Information is a valuable asset when you are aiming for success. Compile as much of it as you can to help you make the right decisions at the beginning of your career and continue to keep your 'market intelligence' up to date to help you make the right decisions in the future.

Working for someone else

A growing area of employment is as an agent, or subcontractor, for someone else. It is in fact self-employment, but in the case of subcontractors, someone else finds the work, and in the case of agents someone else manufactures the products which they sell.

Subcontracting

Subcontracting used to be most common in the building trade. However, it is becoming an increasingly common practice in other trades as well. Gardening is a case in point. Many successful gardening businesses start off as one-man/woman bands and, as they grow, require extra staff. Because the ability to carry out the work is depen-

---

CASE HISTORY: Michael

Michael did a very simple piece of market research. He was an unemployed builder whose speciality was building patios. He therefore rang all the jobbing gardeners in the area and the garden centres that offered gardening services and asked if they provided a patio-building service. If they did not, he asked why, and they usually replied that it was too specialised for them. He then wrote to all those people offering his services as a subcontractor. Many of them took up his offer and began to look for patio work from their regular clients. Business was a little slow at first but now Michael has a steady amount of work.

---

dent on the weather, it is risky to employ others full-time and pay them to do nothing on rainy days, so subcontracting is the answer.

If you are fit and able to turn your hand to any labouring job, whether it is digging a garden, mixing concrete, carrying bricks or cleaning windows, then you should do some research and find out which firms in your area employ subcontractors. You can then make yourself known to a variety of companies and get yourself put on their books for casual work.

If you have a special skill, try to find others with similar skills who have been in operation longer than you and may be in a position to give you some of their overflow work. Alternatively, you might suggest to people with an allied skill that they offer their customers an extra service or product which you can provide when required. This will add an extra dimension to their business without them having to employ another person.

Some examples of this might be:

- You possess binding and laminating machines and you suggest to a typing agency that they offer to bind and laminate their clients' reports. You charge them a price for doing it and they add a bit extra on that price to their clients.
- You are a skilled embroiderer and you suggest to someone who manufactures or sells children's clothes that they could offer a service to their customers whereby clothes are embroidered with the children's names.
- You design and plant up container displays for gardens. You could suggest to local gardening businesses that they purchase ready-made tubs of plants, hanging baskets and so on from you.

Agencies

An agent is a commission-only salesperson who sells products for one or more manufacturers. There are untold numbers of people involved in this type of work, from the women who sell cosmetics, clothing and jewellery through catalogues among friends to the thousands involved in network marketing schemes selling household products.

At the top end of the market are manufacturers' agents represented by the Manufacturers' Agents' Association (MAA).* There are about 20,000 such agents in the UK selling products for both UK and overseas manufacturers. They are mainly people with a professional sales background and a great many contacts which they have built up over the years. This is why the manufacturers are interested in their representation. However, no matter how good their contacts are, they still have to do the kind of research described in this chapter in order to add to their sales and to develop new sales lines.

Anyone wishing to become a manufacturer's agent can contact the MAA, which publishes a newsletter in which manufacturers from all over the world advertise for agents. Also, the various commercial sections of foreign embassies have lists of manufacturers seeking agents. There is also a British Agents Register* which puts agents in touch with manufacturers.

Researching the job market

Finding home-based work of the general kind is not quite so easy. As stated in Chapter 3, there is no list of reputable companies offering homework, according to the National Group on Homeworking.* However, a 'blacklist' has been compiled of companies that have been involved in cheating workers, operating scams or paying dreadful wages. Check with the NGH, a local Homeworking Group or Officer, a Low Pay Unit or your local Trading Standards Department. None of these organisations mentioned can find you homework or provide you with a list of potential employers: finding the work is up to you. However, when you think you have found some work you can check with them to reassure yourself that the employer is reputable.

You could turn to the local newspaper to see if any advertisements are offering work that might suit you. The local JobCentre may have some outwork jobs on offer and the Local Enterprise Agency may have advised recently established businesses who are thinking of employing outworkers or subcontractors.

The National Group on Homeworking recommends the following, in order to find genuine work:

Use your *Yellow Pages* or *Thomson Directory* to identify companies in your area which might put work out to homeworkers. Some examples are: printers, print finishers, direct mail or circular and sample distributors, packers or contract packers, greeting card manufacturers, novelty or carnival goods manufacturers or firms making promotional items, clothing manufacturers, knitwear manufacturers, printed circuit boards and electronic components manufacturers.

These firms will not mention homeworking in their advert but you should telephone the firm and ask if they ever use homeworkers. Try to contact firms near to your home. This will make it easier to deliver and collect work and to deal with any problems.

If the firms you contact say that they do employ homeworkers, ask if they have any work at the moment. If the answer is no, then ask them if you can go on their waiting list and if they know of any other firms that might have some work on offer. Tell them of any relevant experience you may have.

Disabled people can contact the Royal Association for Disability and Rehabilitation (RADAR).★ They publish several useful factsheets and can refer you to other organisations that may have sources of work, such as the Guild of Disabled Homeworkers,★ The Disability Alliance★ and Remploy Ltd.★ Most JobCentres have a Disability Employment Advisor who will be able to advise on the home-based job opportunities that are on offer locally. (See Chapter 3 for more details.)

For teleworkers the market-place is expanding rapidly. Many recruitment agencies now specialise in finding telework jobs for computer specialists, desktop publishing, media, design and advertising personnel. The Telework, Telecottage and Telecentre Association (TCA)★is also a source of job information through its magazine *Teleworker*. It also publishes *The Teleworking Handbook* which has a section on getting work. Many of the trade and computer magazines now carry information about teleworking jobs and more advertisements for such jobs are appearing in the national and industrial press. (Teleworking is discussed in detail in Chapter 3.)

Researching business opportunities

If you are thinking of setting up a business from scratch in England or are trying to research business opportunities generally, contact your nearest Business Link★ facility for information, counselling and advice. Most Business Links offer a mix of free and chargeable services – before arranging counselling services or requesting information about grants from any source, check whether or not a fee is payable. If you live in Scotland, contact Scottish Enterprise.* If you live in Wales, contact Business Connect.*

Regional Arts and Crafts Councils may know whether local artists and craftspeople are looking for partners or investors – you may have a skill that perfectly complements another person's and adds to your business potential, or you may have money and marketing know-how to invest in the right project.

The British Franchise Association* and banks will have information on franchises but, often, the best place to go is to one of the major franchise exhibitions in the UK and have a thorough look at the variety of options on offer. Contact the BFA for details of forthcoming exhibitions.

Whether you are taking over an existing small business or buying a new one, or investing in a franchise, researching its potential and its solidity can really only be done by an accountant and/or your bank.

All the high-street banks now have a franchise department which will investigate and assess a franchise before you buy it, whether the bank is lending you money to purchase or not.

No one should ever buy a business – even a newspaper delivery round – without having a qualified person look at the books and without doing some of the research outlined in this chapter regarding existing and potential markets.

Chapter 5

Money – how to raise it

If you decide to go down the route of self-employment you will need some money behind you, if only to cushion you against the bad weeks when your income is low. You may not need much of an initial investment in stock, materials or equipment but it helps your confidence if you know that you are not completely without money. Of course, you may be in receipt of a state benefit or have some redundancy money or some savings, in which case you will not feel totally penniless. But, for the purposes of this chapter, we will suppose that you need to raise some money in order to get yourself started. This might take the form of:

- money to cover start-up expenses (e.g. equipment)
- finance for the ups and downs of cash flow (e.g. if your cash-flow forecast suggests that you may need to borrow in some months)
- money to buy stock.

Loans and grants are available in certain circumstances, but it should be appreciated from the outset that these are not quick ways of obtaining some start-up money. Bank loans take some time to be approved, loans from government sources and allied bodies take much longer and grants can take forever to come through. So you either have to be prepared to hang on to your full-time job while everything is processed, or you have to borrow the money from a friend or relative on the strength of the grant coming through.

Do not, however difficult it is proving to raise money, borrow money from a money lender who charges horrendous rates of interest. You will cripple your business venture before it even gets off the ground. Similarly, a finance house which charges between

25 and 30 per cent interest per year could prove just too expensive for your fledgling business to sustain. Also, unless you have an interest-free loan or grant confirmed on paper and therefore can definitely pay someone back, do not borrow from friends or relatives if you can help it. Borrowing money is the quickest way to damage a relationship.

Writing your business plan

Until you have worked out how much your product or service will cost to make or provide, what you are going to sell it for and what your estimated outgoings and income will be, you cannot answer the question about whether you need to raise finance.

Cash-flow forecast

You should do a cash-flow forecast first to predict when and where in the year your cash is going to be stretched to the limit and when and where in the year you can expect to generate income. This will show you if you need to borrow money and what form that borrowing might need to take. For example, you may just need an overdraft facility to cover those months when expenditure exceeds income.

A cash-flow forecast not only gives a forecast of expenditure but as you fill in the amounts, it will also give you a historical record of expenditure. The purpose of the cash-flow forecast is to identify heavy months of expenditure so that you can be prepared. The categories would obviously be different to suit your particular business circumstances and, also, the starting month can be at any time of the year. You should fill in the table with actual amounts or estimates. Be generous with the estimates. It is better to find yourself paying less when the time comes than to have budgeted for too little and find yourself short.

You have to draw up a business plan to help you to understand what your financial needs are likely to be and to show to anyone from whom you may be borrowing or receiving money.

A business plan is a concise report which explains your business – what it is and how it will make money – and gives a financial forecast. Local Enterprise Agencies,* Business Links* and banks may be able to help you formulate a business plan but they may charge you for this. Check first. (Business Links are business-led partnerships of all key providers of business support in a locality. They aim to provide help through teams of commercially experienced, independent business advisers and specialist counsellors. In Scotland, contact Scottish Enterprise;* in Wales Business Connect.*)

The first part of the plan should be easy. By now you should have worked through in your mind what you are going to do and how you are going to go about it. You will have decided what product or service you are going to offer, done your research, identified your market and how you are going to sell to that market. This all has to be explained clearly and fully and, preferably, briefly. No one wants to wade through a 20-page report on a small business you are running from your back bedroom; two pages should suffice. In these two pages you need to explain the following. Work through these questions to help you formulate your business plan concisely as you compile the report.

What is your business?

Explain exactly what your product or service is. Do not try to blind anyone with science or use fancy management consultancy jargon. If you are selling cosmetics door-to-door do not call it a health and beauty consultancy. If you are using an umbrella term – for example, you are a teleworker who is running a data management service – explain in the report that this covers creating and amending mailing lists, keeping personnel records, etc., on computer.

Why have you chosen this business?

If it is relevant, outline your past experience in this field, your training and qualifications. If none of that is relevant, and you have just decided on a business because the potential is good and you need no training to be able to operate, explain that too.

What is the market for your product/service?

Explain what your market research has uncovered. If you can throw in a few statistics and name the sources, all the better; it will show that you have done your homework. If you have done a house-to-house survey yourself in your local area, translate that into percentages for the report – for example, out of 54 households interviewed

47 per cent said that they were looking for a window cleaner, 23 per cent already had one, and the rest cleaned their own windows.

Have you identified the competition?

Do you know who else is offering the same product or service and is likely to affect your market? Or have you found a genuine market gap with no competition in sight? Are you sure it is a market gap? Has anyone tried to fill it before and come unstuck? Perhaps the only competition is 100 miles away and will not affect your sales area. Perhaps there is healthy competition but the market is continually growing – for example, you want to set up as a childminder; plenty of other childminders are operating in your area but you have ascertained that the demand is so great that it outstrips the supply.

Why is your product/service better?

Take the example of a children's day nursery. Maybe you want to be better than the others and charge more, so you need to borrow money to put better play equipment in the nursery garden and refurbish the bathrooms. In order for you to arrive at this decision you need to understand what the market wants and to identify what the competition is offering.

How will you reach your customers?

List all the ways in which you want to market your work and how often you would wish to run marketing exercises in the first year. (Marketing your work is covered in detail in Chapter 8.) You need to be able to quote the costs of advertising, leaflet printing, distribution and so on and then add this into your financial forecast, which is part 2 of your business plan (see below). (See also Chapter 10.)

How much can you achieve on your own?

You have to be realistic about your capacity for work and exactly how much revenue you can generate on your own. If you are doing the selling and the paperwork as well you will have only so much time to make your products or provide your service. If you are a craft worker who makes a variety of products, list them and explain how much time it takes to make each one and what the profit margin is.

Product	Time to make	Cost of materials	Selling price
Patchwork cot quilts	3 hours	£5	£20
Patchwork bags	2 hours	£4	£15
Patchwork bed quilts	20 hours	£35	£200

Someone who is considering giving you a loan (your bank manager or Enterprise Agency) may then call in a marketing expert who may advise you that some items are too time-consuming and not cost-effective and that you should concentrate your business efforts on certain products only.

It is important to check with the organisation to which you hope to present your business plan to ascertain whether they have a standard format that they prefer. Some banks, for example, may have forms that they expect you to fill in, rather than presenting your own report.

When will you need to expand?

You may need to use outworkers or take on someone part-time right at the outset or you may be planning to employ someone else, if all goes well, in about a year's time. This needs to be explained in your business plan so that a potential lender can assess your financial needs in the future.

What equipment do you have or need?

You may not have any equipment as such, or you may have old equipment that needs replacing. Perhaps you need to invest in another piece of equipment to allow you to diversify.

Who are or will be your suppliers?

Where do you buy or intend to buy your raw materials? Have you investigated the best prices? Can you get special deals? Anyone considering lending you money will be impressed if you can show that you have investigated all the possibilities.

Cashflow forecast

	Jan	Feb	Mar	Apr	May	Jun	Jul	Aug	Sep	Oct	Nov	Dec
1. Mortgage/rent	•	•	•	•	•	•	•	•	•	•	•	•
2. Council tax	•	•	•	•	•	•	•	•	•	•	•	•
3. Water rates				•						•		
4. Gas		•			•			•			•	
5. Electricity		•			•			•			•	
6. Telephone	•	•		•		•	•		•	•		•
7. HP repayments	•	•	•	•	•	•	•	•	•	•	•	•
8. Equipment rental	•	•	•	•	•	•	•	•	•	•	•	•
9. All insurances			•					•				
10. Loan repayments	•	•	•	•	•	•	•	•	•	•	•	•
11. Car expenses (tax/insurance)		• (Tax)			• (Insurance)			• (Tax)				
12. Car running costs (petrol, service, MOT)				• (Service)						• (Service & MOT)		
13. Purchases of supplies	•	•	•	•	•	•	•	•	•	•	•	•
14. Credit card repayments												
15. Miscellaneous												
16. "												
17. "												
18. Totals												

The financial forecast

Your potential lender will need to know what money is going to go out of your business and what money is going to come in. You only need something simple, such as a cash-flow forecast. If you have a friend or relative who is an accountant, they may be able to help you plot it out. Otherwise a Business Link* adviser will certainly be able to assist you, but there may be a small charge. Check first.

The sales forecast will obviously have a large element of hope involved. You must show if your sales are likely to be seasonal, for example if you make greetings cards and the bulk of your sales are at Christmas. A Christmas card manufacturer may have a lot of cash going out during the first year and not much coming in until the first quarter of the following year.

A cash-flow forecast is a complete breakdown of sources of income as well as expenses. The crucial point about a cash-flow statement is that it shows the timing of receipts and outgoings. It is perfectly possible for a business to look profitable but then fail because of adverse cash flow. Working from home means that you may put down a proportion of your rent/mortgage/Council tax, and bills for light, heat and phone and so forth. You must also consider petrol and car maintenance, if relevant, so that you can sell and deliver your goods. If you are planning to pay any wages during the year, these must be included in your projections. You should also include any up-front investment that needs to be made in equipment or publicity, in order to get you started, as well as any money that will need to be spent later in the year to continue to publicise your business.

This exercise should be done in conjunction with costing your work (see Chapter 7). After you have done these figures you should be able to see whether or not your planned venture will be able to make a profit. If not, you either abandon the idea or see whether you can adapt it.

Decide what type of finance you need. A grant would be ideal, but you may not be able to get one. Perhaps you could get a bank loan or, if you can do without that, an overdraft facility to cover you for those periods when money is going out faster than it comes in.

A bank or an Enterprise Agency will go through the finished plan with you and discuss any weak points before you present it to the ultimate source of finance. It is an important part of your preparation and you must get it right. It is also a document you can build upon and re-present at a later date if you should require further finance to expand or diversify.

Raising some money quickly

Earning money at home is all about careful planning and exercising caution. However, there can be occasions when a business opportunity, vehicle or piece of equipment becomes available and you cannot wait for lengthy financial procedures to be completed. Below are some suggestions how to raise money quickly:

- **Sell something** – you could sell your car and get a cheaper one. You could sell all your unwanted items at a boot fair. That will not raise a lot of money, of course, but it might be enough to help you on your way.
- **Take on a business partner** – this may be a way of borrowing from close relatives without damaging your relationship. Offer them the chance to invest in your enterprise on the understanding that you will run things but they will be kept informed and get a share in any of the profits. If you take this route, however, it will involve you in legal advice and fees, since no partnership should be undertaken without a proper agreement and proper safeguards in place.
- **Hire purchase** – this is a good way of getting some essential equipment for your enterprise, if such an arrangement is available. Only opt for *bona fide* hire-purchase agreements, after thoroughly investigating the true cost involved. Can you afford the monthly repayments? It is vital to establish this first.
- **Interest-free credit** – this may be available on certain items such as sewing machines, knitting machines or computers. In the current competitive climate, you can get some good bargains, provided you are able to pay the initial deposit and either keep up the monthly payments or pay the outstanding money at the end of the credit period.
- **Credit card** – buying items of equipment on a credit card will give you up to 56 days interest free before the bill must be paid; after that you can, if you wish, pay in instalments. It is an expen-

sive way to buy as the interest rates are high if you do not settle the whole sum when you get the bill. But in the short term this form of credit can still be cheaper than a bank overdraft.

- **Second mortgage on the house** – this will take a little longer to arrange and it is risky to tie your house up in your business venture because you could lose it. Anyway, if you are self-employed, and not a company, your personal assets are already at risk, as you do not have limited liability. Getting a loan against the value of your house depends on whether the lender thinks you can afford more monthly repayments and the size of your mortgage, if any. If you have paid off your mortgage and own your house, then you will be able to get a substantial loan. If you have only paid off the interest on your mortgage and not yet paid off any of the capital, then you will probably not be able to get a loan.

- **Surrender a life insurance policy** – only certain policies can be surrendered, i.e. investment-type policies which pay you bonuses along the way, adding up to a nice nest egg when the policy has run its term. A policy has to have built up a surrender value, which usually takes a number of years. The younger the policy, the less you are likely to get back if you surrender it – you will certainly not get back what you paid in in premiums. However, if the policy is older, and a good number of bonuses have built up, you may get back more than you have paid in. If you surrender a policy, you will lose out on the terminal bonus, which is often quite generous. This is not a recommended course to take as, usually, surrender values are very low.

- **Borrow against an insurance policy** – this form of loan against policies from insurers has become very competitive but you have to have a suitable policy – again, an investment-type policy that is reasonably mature and one that is not linked to your mortgage. Insurers seem to prefer a long-term loan, such as three to five years or over. The current rates of interest (autumn 1998) are very good, on average about nine per cent APR (Annual Percentage Rate – the amount of interest charged in one year) – much better than bank or building society loans or overdrafts. You have to keep up the policy premiums, though, as well as repaying the loan. If you have a policy which is, say, seven years off maturity, it is a good way of releasing some funds early because you know that at the end of the seven-year period, when the policy comes to term, you should still have a profit.

Special loans, grants and bursaries

Ideally, you should have planned your work-at-home career sufficiently to be able to have saved some money to start yourself off. It is important that you keep all the money for and relating to your fledgling business in a separate account from your personal money. This does not have to be a business account to start off with, as the charges on such accounts are steep. However, if you are starting an ambitious enterprise which will require applying for loans or over-draft facilities you will, undoubtedly, have to open a business account with your lender.

At least allow yourself time to start up, so that you are not in a position of having to raise cash quickly. If you have planned ahead, you may be able to apply for one of the grants or loans that are currently available. Finding out what is available requires a little research. Librarians should be able to access up-to-date grant information via their online databases. (There are all kinds of grants on offer in the European Union (EU) but they come and go with alarming rapidity.) If you have access to the Internet you can find all the information you need by looking through DTI or European Social Fund databases or similar. Also, your Local Enterprise Agency (LEA),★ Training and Enterprise Council (TEC)★ or Local Enterprise Company (LEC) in Scotland, or Business Link will be able to tell you what, if anything, your venture might be able to gain.

It is not possible to list in this book all the grants and loans available in the UK and EU. Below are the ones most likely to be of interest to the individual just starting out.

Bear in mind that the availability and size of grants change all the time because they are controlled by government policy regarding public sector largesse.

Government help

Loan Guarantee Scheme
The DTI's Small Firms Loan Guarantee Scheme provides a government guarantee for loans by approved lenders. Loans are to

firms or individuals unable to obtain conventional finance because of a lack of security. The guarantee generally covers 70 per cent of the outstanding loan. This rises to 85 per cent for established businesses trading two years or more. Loans are generally for amounts between £5,000 and £100,000 (£250,000 for established businesses) and over a period of two to ten years. Not all types of businesses are eligible for loans and the use of loans is restricted. Check the details with your LEA.

LINC

A number of LEAs have jointly set up the Local Investment Networking Company (LINC). LINC is a nation-wide introduction service between investors and small businesses seeking start-up growth capital. They are, in principle, willing to sell a proportion of their equity to the investor. Your LEA can explain how the service works. Contact your Business Link, TEC or the National Federation of Enterprise Agencies* for details of the nearest LEA.

Enterprise Investment Scheme

The Enterprise Investment Scheme (EIS) has been introduced to help small, unquoted trading companies raise equity finance and to encourage 'business angels' (outside investors who contribute both capital and management expertise) to invest in these companies.

Venture Capital Trusts

Venture Capital Trusts (VCTs) are quoted limited companies whose purpose is to invest shareholders' funds in smaller unquoted trading companies. VCTs will provide a new source of finance for both new and expanding businesses.

Regional Selective Assistance and Enterprise Grants

On 1 April 1997 the Regional Enterprise Grant Scheme (REG) was combined with Regional Selective Assistance (RSA) and a then new SMART/SPUR/SPURplus scheme (The Small Firms Merit Award for Research & Technology/ Support For Products Under Research). This grant is discussed later in the chapter. Discretionary RSA grants are available to assist projects that either create new jobs or protect existing jobs in those parts of the UK designated as Assisted Areas, such as former coal mining towns. REG will only be available to projects in the East and West Midlands coal closure areas which fall outside the Assisted Areas. This scheme provides fixed grants to smaller firms proposing new capital investment. Firms may apply for a grant covering 15 per cent of the cost of fixed assets of a project up to a maximum grant of £15,000.

Rural areas

Most of the grants or loans available for rural areas are concerned with diversification of land or turning a redundant building into a business enterprise and are covered fully in Chapter 12.

Small Firms Training Loans

These are available through the Department for Education and Employment (DfEE) and seven major banks to help businesses who employ from 1 to 50 people to pay for vocational education or training. The Training Loans Scheme offers deferred repayment terms.

* Firms can borrow between £500 and £125,000 to cover training costs and, subject to a maximum loan of £5,000, consultancy advice on training matters.
* Any education or training course, whether full-time, part-time, in-house or distance learning is eligible as long as small firms can show that it will help them achieve their business objectives.
* Those eligible to apply are any business already trading or about to trade with 1 to 50 permanent employees or any sole traders, business partnerships, co-operatives, franchises and limited companies.
* There is nothing to pay for up to 12 months of training. The DfEE pays the interest for this period.
* The loan is repaid over a minimum period of one year up to a maximum of seven years.

Career Development Loans

These deferred payment loans help individuals, including business owners, pay for vocational training courses lasting no longer than two years plus, if relevant, a maximum of one year's practical experience, where it is part of the course. The government pays the interest on the loan for the duration of the course, which is administered through one of four major high-street banks, and for up to one month afterwards. The borrower then repays the loan and any further interest over a period agreed by the bank.

Training for Work Scheme

People who have been unemployed for more than 12 months may wish to opt for the Training for Work Scheme. It is possible under this programme for an individual to receive training and financial support to assist their move into self-employment. Information is available through local JobCentres.

Assistance for the unemployed to start businesses

Some TECs and LECs may provide financial support to unemployed people who wish to start up their own small business. It varies from region to region so check with your local centre.

Help with skills and technology

Listed below are some grant schemes geared towards research and development. A lone inventor, or a very small hi-tech company working from home may be eligible for these schemes.

The Teaching Company Scheme

The TCS is run by the Teaching Company Directorate* and helps businesses of all sizes, but especially small firms with potential for growth, to access the knowledge, skills and technology in UK universities through partnerships between academia and business. A TCS programme involves one or more graduates each working for two years on key technology transfer projects identified by the company. For small firms, 70 per cent of the cost of using a graduate's skills can be awarded in grant form, and the remaining 30 per cent has to be found by the firm itself.

SMART

SMART (it stands for Small firms Merit Award for Research and Technology) is an annual competition for individuals and businesses with less than 50 employees. It provides grants of up to £45,000 to help with the costs of technical and feasibility studies into innovative technology. Winners may receive further assistance under SPUR (see below) to develop a prototype.

SPUR

Support for Products Under Research or SPUR provides grants of up to £162,000 for the development of new products and processes which involve a significant technological advance. It is particularly geared towards small businesses.

Export support

Advice on exporting is available to any lone entrepreneur or small company wishing to export goods or services from Business Link★ in England. In Scotland contact Scottish Enterprise.★ In Wales contact Business Connect.★

Special funding is available for companies who want to operate in Central and Eastern Europe. The European Investment Bank also finances loans to small and medium enterprises. The European Investment Fund underwrites loans to small firms. Information is available from European Information Centres.★ There is also The Export Award for Smaller Businesses. Any small firm that exports goods or services can apply. Each recipient gets £5,000 and valuable professional advice.

Other sources of grants and loans

The Prince's Youth Business Trust and the Prince's Scottish Youth Business Trust*

These two organisations help unemployed young people aged between 18 and 30 to start their own businesses by providing financial help, business monitoring and marketing opportunities. Applicants must have a viable business idea and be able to demonstrate the necessary initiative and commitment to make it succeed and they must have been unable to obtain funding from other sources.

The Trust will award a loan of up to a maximum of £5,000 to a person starting a business. Beneficial repayment terms of three per cent per £1,000 per annum over a one- to three-year period are available, and there are no repayments for the first six months. Business expansion loans are also available for people under the age of 30 who have already received a loan or a bursary. The total of all loans for one individual or small business may not exceed £5,000. The Trust also offers bursaries of up to £1,500 to individuals or

£3,000 to groups in exceptional circumstances. Test Marketing Grants (up to £250) are available to help applicants assess if there is a market for their product or service.

Highlands & Islands Enterprise*

This organisation is interested in assisting the social and economic development, training and environmental renewal in the Highlands and Islands, which covers half of Scotland. Grant provision varies but is quite generous, and the HIE is particularly interested in emerging businesses in the areas of food and drink, manufacturing and production, tourism and IT and telecoms.

Livewire*

Sponsored by Shell UK Ltd, Livewire offers advice and assistance on business start-up and planning. This is for young entrepreneurs aged between 16 and 25. Livewire also holds an annual competition to reward the achievements of young people new to business. Winners receive cash awards.

The Crafts Council*

Grants are available nationally to assist chosen craft workers, of any age, to set up their first workshop. The grant is in two parts: a maintenance grant of £2,500 for one year; and a grant for 50 per cent of the cost of purchasing or hiring equipment up to a maximum of £5,000. Applicants may apply up to two years after setting up. There are four deadlines each year for applications: 1 March, 1 June, 1 September, 1 December.

The Arts Councils* (National and Regional)

Grants are available for both individuals and organisations. The Arts Councils of England, Scotland and Wales tend to reserve their grant aid for projects of national or international significance. Regional and local councils have a budget and they decide on their own local priorities. If you think you might stand a chance, put in an application. Remember, too that Arts Councils cover all the visual and performing arts.

Tourist Boards

Many of the grants and loans available for tourist projects are discussed in Chapter 12. However, not everyone wants to start up a tourist business using their own home and land. In certain areas, such as Wales and Scotland, there is a general policy to encourage tourism as much as possible and therefore new or potential businesses are more likely to get financial support, particularly if they will employ others. Detailed information on the kind of support available can be obtained from the regional Tourist Boards or through Enterprise Agencies.

Private sector finance

Most business start-ups approach the high-street banks first, although many building societies are now offering similar financial services. Remember that these institutions do not lend money without some sort of guarantee that they will get it back in one way or another. This usually means some form of security against the loan (unless you are able to get on the government's Loan Guarantee Scheme, see page 90). Whether this is necessary will depend on the size and type of the loan, for example security would not normally be required for a small overdraft facility. The security demanded is usually one of the following:

A mortgage on your home

If you default on the loan the bank has a right to sell your home to get its money back. However, it is unlikely that the bank will want your home as security unless you are borrowing a very large amount of money. The size of the loan allowed will depend upon how much your house is worth when any outstanding mortgage is subtracted. Before putting your house forward as security against the loan, discuss it thoroughly with your spouse/partner/family. It is not recommended for those with a nervous disposition.

A life insurance policy

A life insurance policy with a substantial surrender value of more than the value of the loan is signed over to the bank for the period of the loan. In the event of the borrower's death the bank will be automatically repaid and any balance will be handed over to the family. In the event of default, the bank will surrender the policy and reclaim its money. You have to keep up the premiums on the policy, of course. This is a good way to secure a loan and does not threaten your home at all. Make sure you have enough life insurance cover so that your family will not be penniless if you die. Term life insurance is the cheapest and, as it has no investment value, it cannot be used as security for a loan.

Stocks and shares

A block of shares worth considerably more than the value of the loan (because of the fluctuating nature of the market) can be signed over to the bank for the period of the loan. As with the life insurance policy, should you default on the loan or die, the bank sells the stocks and shares. This is also a popular way of securing a loan because it does not risk your home and you do get the stocks and shares back after you have paid off the loan.

A personal guarantee

This is a written guarantee from a third party stating that he or she will pay off the loan if the borrower cannot. Banks will rarely accept this as total security (unless your guarantor is a multi-millionaire) and will probably ask for one of the above (insurance policy, stocks and shares, etc.) to be given by the guarantor as a back up. The guarantor should be fully aware of the risks involved in acting as guarantor for someone.

What the banks can offer

Most lending institutions will expect you to bank with them if you want financial help. However, if your existing bank will not give you a loan or is not offering an attractive package, there is no reason why you cannot apply to other institutions and offer to move your account if they will help.

Overdrafts

An overdraft is an agreement with the bank that the bank will let you overdraw your account up to a set sum. It is a useful way of borrowing money in the short term to finance the difficult cash-flow periods. It is, however, not the best way of borrowing money as there will probably be several charges incurred – to set up the facility, a monthly administration charge and, of course, high charges should you exceed the overdraft limit or not repay on time. The interest charged will be linked to the bank base rate and so it will vary and overdrafts are usually reviewed every twelve months unless the customer is causing problems and the bank feels obliged to review the situation before the end of the agreed term.

Short-term loans

The banks usually classify 'short-term' as up to two years. Rates of interest vary from bank to bank and can be fixed or can fluctuate with the base rate. Fixed-rate loans are where the interest is fixed i.e. does not fluctuate, for an agreed period (it is rarely for the whole term of the loan). It is worth shopping around to see which lender offers the best deal. For financing the purchase of equipment a short-term loan usually works out cheaper than hire purchase or leasing, but investigate thoroughly because you may be able to get a cheaper deal on hire purchase through an arrangement made by your local trade association or other body of which you are a member.

One vital difference between a loan and hire purchase is that once you have bought a piece of equipment with a loan it is yours completely, whereas when you obtain a piece of equipment through hire purchase it is not yours until the last payment has been made and, therefore, could be repossessed if you do not keep up the payments.

Medium-term loans

These may span up to ten years and repayments are usually flexible in that they can be scheduled to suit the demands of your business. If, for example, you are in a seasonal business where you receive the bulk of your income at a particular point in the year you can schedule repayments for that time each year. To attract customers, many lenders offer incentives such as 'repayment holidays', meaning that no repayments are made for the first two years of the life of the loan. These are especially useful for business start-ups, but the banks do not lose out and the higher repayments later on have to be built into your financial forecasts.

Long-term loans

These are of over ten years' duration. They are unlikely to be of interest to the home-based business as they are commonly used to buy fixed assets with a long life span, such as buildings or large pieces of machinery. If you need to buy a bigger house in order to work from home, a conventional mortgage is much cheaper than a long-term loan.

Commercial mortgages

If you want to buy a property that will become your business as well as your home – a nursing home or shop, for example – you can take out a commercial mortgage. They are usually for a shorter period than domestic mortgages, requiring, say, a ten- to fifteen-year repayment rather than twenty or twenty-five years. Lending institutions say that they currently take each application on its merits and it is possible to negotiate deals similar to domestic mortgages, with low initial repayments, endowments attached and so on. It all depends on the size of the loan, whether the business is new or existing and several other factors.

There is tax relief on this form of mortgage and no upper limit on the size of the loan. Many lenders offer incentives in the form of 'repayment holidays' for the first year or so. Payments can be made monthly or quarterly and interest can be fixed or variable; you can usually opt to review your choice of interest status every year. Security for the finance is given by signing over the deeds of the property to the lenders so that in the event of default they can sell the property and reclaim their money. They will probably also require insurances to be taken out.

Chapter 6

Organising yourself

It is important that your home does not turn into a complete tip, with explosions of paperwork or manufacturing-in-progress everywhere. Try to make one particular place your work base. This does not mean that you cannot sit in front of the television during the day or in the evening doing your envelope stuffing/embroidery/dried flower arrangements and so on, but it does mean that you should have a room or a cupboard where everything is put away when you are not doing it. And, if you have small children, that place should preferably have a lock on it for their safety and your sanity – you do not want to find the kids tinkering with your computer when your back is turned and wiping out all your records! However, try not to make one part of your house exclusively for work, as you may find yourself liable to pay business rates. (Storing away dangerous or valuable equipment in a lockable room is different.)

The place where you work

The place you set aside for most of your work should be comfortable, the temperature should be adjustable, there should be some natural light and good ventilation. In your enthusiasm at starting your own venture you may think that you can happily work in a damp cellar, a draughty attic or a cold shed, but after a few weeks the reality will begin to get you down.

If you intend to do a lot of office work, you will require a proper office set-up. You will need space to lay out all your papers; a suitable desk and comfortable, adjustable but supportive chair (you don't want to get backache or stiff shoulders and neck); somewhere to file all your documents; a telephone near at hand (you cannot keep running up and down stairs every time it rings; perhaps it is time to think about a mobile or a cordless phone); and peace and quiet if the job at hand requires concentration.

If you are manufacturing, repairing, renovating, or raising plants in your outbuildings, you need some space and a source of power for your tools and to provide warmth and light. Someone in the house may answer the phone for you but it might be useful to have an extension in the shed or a cordless telephone. The outbuilding should be waterproof and easily heated.

You may be able to do work such as hand-knitting anywhere, but you need a place to store all your materials. This should be dry, animal/insect/children-proof and easy to get at – you do not want to have to bring out a ladder and climb up into the roof every time you want a box of wool.

Organising yourself for work is basically common sense but sometimes the enthusiasm of starting this new career prevents a calm assessment of the true picture. You can work successfully only if you have the space and you have prepared your working conditions properly.

Keeping accounts

As discussed in Chapter 5, it is imperative to keep all your business monies in a separate bank or building society account so that you can keep track of your income and expenditure and do not get them mixed up with your domestic monies. You must also inform the Contributions Agency and Inland Revenue if you become self-employed.

It is important to keep a careful record of all financial transactions concerned with your work, not only to check whether you are making a profit or loss but also because the Inland Revenue and Customs and Excise can ask at any time to see past accounts from six years previously, or longer if they suspect fraud.

As soon as you start to earn or pay out any money at all, keep a record of all expenses and payments as they arise. Make sure that the full date is on everything. Fill in cheque stubs and paying-in slips clearly and fully.

A simple ruled cash book may be enough to start with: on one side enter what you have earned and on the other enter expenses, with dates and any other relevant details. Keep distinct records of cash and banking transactions. All money received (cash and cheques) should be paid in, even if you withdraw it again immediately. You must keep all receipts, till slips, invoices, etc., so that an auditor can check them against your accounts.

Your volume of work will dictate what records need to be kept. For instance, a writer whose year's work produces, say, one book may just have a single receipt of payment from the publisher with few expenses – perhaps paper, floppy disks, postage, fares. On the other hand, someone offering hairdressing will have numerous small receipts of cash and expenses for stock, equipment and telephone, a car if he or she travels to clients and will need a more elaborate cash book for payments, VAT records and so on.

It is wise to write up your account books at least once a week. Where applicable, the following should be recorded, with dates:

- payments made for stock
- payments made for other purchases or services
- money received and from whom
- goods or services supplied and from whom
- cash drawn for personal use.

Although records can be simple, they must be comprehensive and capable of providing information for income tax purposes and for VAT (or, if VAT registration is not yet required, capable of being adapted later to provide the necessary information).

If you decide that more elaborate records are necessary, go to a stationery or office equipment shop and examine the cash record books and account books available. A loose-leaf analysis book with, say, four columns for receipts and 16 columns for payments enables you to keep a cumulative check on how your venture is proceeding (with a cross-check for arithmetical accuracy) and also provides the figures you may need for submission to a bank manager, accountant, Inland Revenue and Customs and Excise (for VAT). Many accountants recommend using something like a Simplex D cash book. Or, if you have a computer, you could choose one of the many accounting software packages. Remember to keep a copy of all computer accounts in a separate place, in case of theft or fire.

Useful computer financial packages

For the small business TAS Books (Megatech Software), Quick Books (Intuit), Sage Instant Accounts (Sage), Money Manager (Connect Software) and Pegasus Solo Accounting (Pegasus) are all excellent account packages. Many can be combined with extra modules to add features such as full reporting, job costing and so on.

For domestic users the most popular packages are Money (Microsoft), Quicken (Intuit).

Popular tax planners include QuickTax (Intuit) and the Consumers' Association's own tax-planning software, TaxCalc, which is updated annually.

The most widely used spreadsheets include the immensely powerful Lotus 1-2-3 (Lotus) and Excel (Microsoft).

File all your invoices, bills, copies of receipts given, cheque stubs, letters and anything else at all relating to your takings and expenditure in date order. If there are not many, they can be put into a folder or box file or on a spike; alternatively, keep them in a ring binder, numbered and cross-referenced to your account books.

It is a good idea to separate the papers for each accounting year so that when you come to make your declaration of income for tax purposes, you will have all the relevant material to hand and will not have to go ferreting among all your bills and letters to find out how much you earned in a particular year. Keep everything for at least six years; the Inland Revenue (and Customs and Excise) have the right to examine your records at any time and you are obliged to produce relevant information on demand.

Always make a note of any item that might possibly be allowable for tax purposes. It is difficult to get a claim allowed for any items if they have not been recorded in the business books.

Be especially careful to record all expenses that relate to your work where part of your business expenses come out of the household account, such as electricity or telephone bills. You will need some record of all such expenses when compiling a claim for tax allowances.

The money that comes in and goes out for your work should be kept strictly separate from your personal and household finances. You could have two cheque books and paying-in books, using one for business and one for private payments, or you could simply mark all personal transactions in the accounts – say as 'drawings' for items of personal expenditure – if you are self-employed.

You could open a separate bank or Girobank account for your business finances, or an instant access building society account. (But make sure you do not pay two lots of bank charges – most banks charge for each transaction unless you keep your current account in credit to a certain sum.) Even if you are just a personal account holder you are entitled to ask for regular monthly statements, or more frequent ones if you wish, although you will be charged for any service that is not standard. Check at regular intervals that the balance of your account agrees with your account books.

If you set up a limited company, the law requires that you have a business account. If you are starting off modestly as a sole trader or are self-employed then you do not have to have a business account, as they can prove expensive for someone building up gradually into a business. It is worth mentioning that, later on, when you have expanded and want to transfer your funds into a business account, the charges are an allowable business expense as far as the Inland Revenue is concerned.

It is essential to set aside in a savings deposit account the money required to meet tax and VAT liabilities when these fall due. You do not want to be faced with a staggering tax or VAT bill with no money available to pay it.

Employing an accountant

Even though a system of self-assessment of tax liabilities now operates in the UK and the Inland Revenue offers a free advice and support service for the procedure, many self-employed people find it worthwhile to get an accountant or book-keeper to advise them on the best method of keeping proper accounts and how to claim any expenses allowable against tax. Personal recommendation is generally the safest way of finding such an adviser. If you do not know of one your bank manager or solicitor may be able to suggest someone. Accountants advertise their services in the local press and in the *Yellow Pages* and local trade directories. Or you can find out the address of your nearest district society of chartered or certified accountants from the local library. The society will be able to give you the names of qualified accountants in your area and may even be able to offer advice about particular accountants' specialities.

When first contacting a firm of accountants, make it clear that you need somebody who knows about the financial aspects of a self-employed or freelance person. An accountant knowledgeable about the hazards and complexities of self-employment can save you a lot of money as well as time; one who specialises in a different area may be unaware of all the pitfalls and possibilities.

Professional accountants charge on an hourly basis, according to seniority and type of work, plus expenses. There is no fixed scale, but allow for at least £35 an hour, plus VAT. Specify (preferably in writing) what work you want an accountant to do for you and ask what his or her charge is likely to be. The bill should be itemised according to the work you have agreed between you – for example, giving advice, preparing a tax return, dealing with VAT and any other book-keeping matters. Obviously, the more thorough you are in your method of book-keeping, the less work an accountant has to do and the more money it will save you.

The accounting year

With the possible exception of the first year, your accounts should run for a 12-month period which begins and ends on the same dates each year. Your accounting year need not necessarily be the calendar year 1 January to 31 December, nor need it coincide with the tax year 6 April to 5 April.

Because of the way in which self-employed tax assessments are made, substantial tax advantages or disadvantages can result from the selection of the annual accounting date.

If you choose your accounting year carefully, i.e. end it a little after the start of the tax year, you will maximise the period of time between making the profits and paying the final instalment of tax due on them. As long as your profits are rising, this is an advantage, as you will be paying tax on lower profits than you are currently making. Take advice from your accountant and/or refer to *Which? Way to Save Tax* (a book published annually by Which? Books) or *The Which? Tax-Saving Guide* (issued with *Which?* magazine in March every year).

T

Record all business receipts and earnings

These must include:

- all money earned, but not necessarily received, by the main activity of the business, that is the provision of goods and services
- all tips, commissions, discounts or rebates
- the normal selling price of any goods or materials you took out of the business for your own use or for your family and friends, or donated to charity or competitions
- the value of any goods or services you received in exchange for work done or goods sold
- any grant, allowance, subsidy or bursary you receive.

Record all day-to-day expenditure

This includes:

- purchases of stock
- rent, heat, light, phone
- insurances
- running costs of a car, van or other vehicle
- printing, photocopying, faxes, stationery, delivery costs and postage, computer software
- staff, outworker or subcontractor wages or payments.

Record all capital expenditure

This includes:

Tax

The Inland Revenue has a range of publications that cover many aspects of tax and most types of business, from keeping livestock to renting rooms. A free catalogue of leaflets and booklets is available.

Submitting accounts

Annual accounts will usually have to be submitted to the tax inspector, giving details of your trading profit. Individuals and partnerships (not companies) who have an annual turnover of less than a certain amount (at the time of writing it is £15,000 per year) may cklist

- any plant or machinery you have purchased for your work
- vans, cars, motor bikes and so on
- furniture and fittings
- computer hardware, fax machines, telephones, word processors and so on
- other equipment, for example scaffolding, ladders, buckets, wheelbarrows.

Record the details of the purchase and sale of capital equipment

If you are buying equipment, the Inland Revenue will want to know the following:

- what did you buy?
- when did you buy it?
- how much did it cost?
- what proportion is used for business purposes? (a telephone, for example, may have a domestic use as well.)

If you sell equipment the Inland Revenue will want to know:

- what you sold
- when did you sell it?
- how much did you receive in cash or part-exchange?

submit a simple three-line summary to the tax office, if they wish. The turnover is the gross or full amount your business earns before deducting any running expenses.

For example:

Turnover	£13,847
Less business expenses	£3,017
Net profits	£10,830

The Inland Revenue reserves the right to ask for more details if, for example, your turnover has suddenly done a nosedive to a low figure when previously you were earning far more. However, the simple tax account is usually acceptable, particularly in the case of people just starting up.

If you are genuinely self-employed, you will be taxed under Schedule D. This may allow you to claim tax relief on more expenses than if you were an employee and taxed by PAYE under Schedule E and also means that you pay less National Insurance. It is important that the Inland Revenue has accepted your self-employed status, because if it has not some of your clients might make you pay employer's contributions.

To be considered self-employed, you have to prove to the Inland Revenue's satisfaction that no one person has the sole rights to your working time. Therefore, try to get work from several sources.

Whether you are employed or self-employed depends on the terms of the particular engagement you have entered into. If you supply a service to only one, or predominantly one customer, a formal letter or contract might clarify your position as an independent self-employed contractor.

Allowable expenses

The Inland Revenue defines an allowable expense as 'any expense which is wholly, necessarily and exclusively incurred for the purpose of the trade' but some items are allowed if a 'proportion' of their use is for your business, for example, premises, cars, telephone. In other words the following:

Stock and services
Things or people's services (as in the case of an agency) that you buy and then resell.

Accommodation costs
A proportion of your rent, business rates (note that it is the whole amount of business rates and a proportion of domestic rates or Council Tax), heating, lighting, telephone, water and any alterations or repairs carried out to the 'business' part of your home, for example an artist might have a bigger window installed in his or her studio to give more light.

The Inland Revenue leaflet (IR56/NI39) *Employed or Self-Employed? A Guide for tax and National Insurance* offers the following checklist:

If you can answer 'yes' to the following questions, you are probably an employee

- Do you yourself have to do the work rather than hire someone else to do it for you?
- Can someone tell you at any time what to do or when and how to do it?
- Are you paid by the hour, week or month? Can you get overtime pay?
- Do you work set hours, or a given number of hours a week or month?
- Do you work at the premises of the person you work for, or at a place or places he or she decides?

If you can answer 'yes' to the following questions, you are probably self-employed

- Do you have the final say in how the business is run?
- Do you risk your own money in the business?
- Are you responsible for meeting the losses as well as taking the profits?
- Do you provide the main items of equipment you need to do your job, not just the small tools many employees provide for themselves?
- Are you free to hire other people on your own terms to do the work you have taken on? And do you pay them out of your own pocket?
- Do you have to correct unsatisfactory work at your own time and at your own expense?

If you are in any doubt, both the Contributions Agency and the Inland Revenue will advise you over the telephone.

Employee costs
Wages/salaries, pensions, insurances and employers' NI contributions.

Marketing
Advertising, sales promotions, public relations – anything under these headings. This also includes any 'free' gifts to clients/customers provided they are not in the form of alcohol, tobacco or food, that they advertise your company (for example calendars or diaries with your company name on) and that they do not exceed £15 each in cost. Also included are the materials you may purchase in respect of market research, such as publications or surveys.

Bad debts
Monies that you cannot recover from customers, that is, specific bad debts.

Finance
Interest on any bank loans, bank charges, hire purchase or leasing contracts.

VAT
If you are not registered for VAT, the VAT you pay on the goods and services that you buy is treated as an allowable expense.

Pre-trading expenses
Any money spent on research, setting-up costs and so on.

Others
Transport, travel, hotels, training costs (if incurred after business start-up), stationery, postage, professional services such as accountants and solicitors, insurances.

Non-allowable expenses

Entertaining
Taking customers for a meal; hospitality of any kind (although entertaining staff is allowed).

Excluded professional fees
The costs of forming a company, architect's fees or the costs of drawing up a lease, for example.

Clothing
Unless your occupation demands special protective clothing or uniforms.

Depreciation
This is not an expense allowance. However, you claim capital allowances in respect of the purchase of plant, machinery, equipment and premises.

Fines
Any fines incurred through the legal process, including parking tickets.

Non-taxable income

Redundancy payments
Anything below £30,000 is tax free.

State benefits
This is of particular relevance to disabled and retired people. See Chapter 3, which contains details of non-taxable benefits.

National Insurance
The principal national insurance rates for 1998/9 are detailed in the table below:

Class 1 – not contracted out	Employer % of all earnings	Employee
Weekly earning bands		
£64 – £109.99	3.0	)
£110 – £154.99	5.0	) 2% of the first £64
£155 – £209.99	7.0	) (i.e.£1.28) plus 10%
£210 – £485	10.0	) of remainder
Over £485	10.0	£43.38 max.
Men 65 and over and women aged 60 and over	as above	Nil
Class 1A – on car and fuel benefits	10.0	Nil

Class 2 – self employed limit of net earnings for exception	£6.35 per week £3,590 pa
Class 3 – voluntary	£6.25 per week
Class 4* – self employed on profits £7,310 –£25,220	6% £1,074.60 max.

*Exemption applies if pensionable age is reached by 6 April 1998

It is possible for a person to be in the situation of being both employed and self-employed, for example as an employed teleworker but doing some freelance work on the side, in which case Class 1 and 2 contributions together will be limited to no more than the maximum contributions an employee would pay. But you may have to pay Class 4 contributions on top of this. Get advice from your local Contributions Agency office (the address will be in your local *Yellow Pages*).

Exemptions

The self-employed are exempt from paying National Insurance contributions if:

- they are in receipt of maternity allowance
- they are sick for a prolonged period
- they have reached pensionable age
- earnings for that year are below a certain limit.

It is worth noting that Class 4 contributions are related to profits and if you should make a loss in any taxable year you will not pay Income Tax or Class 4 contributions.

It is always advisable to check with the Contributions Agency if you are in any doubt about the contributions you should be making and to read their literature before starting your venture or seeking work.

VAT

Registration for VAT is compulsory if your sales for the preceding 12 months or your anticipated sales for the next 12 months are over the current VAT threshold of £50,000. Some traders register voluntarily for VAT even though their sales do not come above the threshold because it is advantageous for them to be able to reclaim the VAT they pay out on supplies.

For example, even if you are supplying goods or services which are zero-rated (which means that you do not charge VAT to your customers), then, by registering, you will be able to claim back the VAT on all your business expenses on which VAT is charged. If you register before you start trading you can reclaim VAT on pre-trading business expenses (see Cash Accounting, below).

The VAT that you pay on your purchases is called 'input tax' and the VAT you charge on goods or services you sell is called 'output tax'. The difference between the two is what is paid to the Customs and Excise. In other words, you buy an item from a company which costs £1.00 plus 0.18p VAT. You then sell that item on to your customer for £2.00 plus 0.35p VAT. The VAT that you then pay to Customs and Excise is 35p – 18p = 17p, the difference between the two.

Most goods and services are classed as standard rate VAT, which is currently 17.5 per cent in the UK. Some goods and services are exempt, for example, finance and education. (Check with Customs and Excise★ for a detailed list.)

Some goods and services are zero rated, for example children's clothing and food (but not catering services). Again, consult Customs and Excise for a detailed list.

There is a reduced rate of VAT (5 per cent) and this is limited to domestic fuel and power.

If you register for VAT you have to give customers a detailed invoice, showing a complete breakdown of the transaction. Most people, once they have had detailed invoice paper printed and set up a system, do it for every sale whether it is over £100 or not.

By law, the invoice must show the following:

- your business names and address
- your VAT registration number
- your invoice number
- either the date of invoice, date of supply, or date of receipt of payment (this is called the 'tax point')
- customer's name and address
- manner of supply, i.e. rent, sale, lease
- description of goods or services supplied

- quantity or period of supply, e.g. 6 lawnmowers or 1 temporary typist for three days
- cost of those goods or that service
- the amount of VAT on each item
- the rate of VAT on each item, i.e. 17.5 per cent
- any discounts given
- the total cost (excluding VAT)
- the separate total VAT
- the grand total.

Note: no tax invoice is necessary for sales direct to the public, for example in a shop or market, unless the customer insists.

If you are registered for VAT but just want to reclaim VAT on purchases, you have to keep all the relevant invoices of purchases made and they should, preferably, show a complete breakdown of how the VAT was arrived at. If you opt to do monthly returns, rather than quarterly, as is the norm, you are reimbursed more speedily for monies paid out. If, however, you do not wish to do the paperwork every month, make any sizeable purchases just before the end of the quarter. If you make them just after you have submitted your quarterly return then you will, in effect, be waiting six months for reimbursement, not three. A third possibility would be to go for annual accounting: the advantage of this is that you send in just one VAT return a year, but on the minus side you have a long wait for repayment if you have overpaid VAT through the nine monthly estimated payments. Discuss the options with your accountant.

Those who are registered should only send out invoices after the end of the quarter. This means that you have three months in which to collect payment from your customers before you in turn have to pay Customs and Excise.

Working from home, you can claim back a proportion of VAT on such items as the telephone bill and petrol for your vehicle. The amount you can claim back is decided by Customs and Excise.

If you go for quarterly returns it is very important that they are submitted within one month of the end of the quarter. Failure to do so can result in, at the least, interest being charged on the late payment and, at the worst, a heavy fine. There are also severe penalties for any 'misdeclarations' or attempts to falsify VAT returns.

Cash accounting

Normally, VAT is due on the invoices you send out, even if you have to wait some time for payment. But, fortunately, most small businesses or sole traders can (and should) opt for the cash accounting system by which to pay VAT. This means that the tax point is the date when money is received from customers, not the date when you asked them for the money. This greatly assists the cash-flow problems of small businesses because it means that you do not have to pay Customs and Excise the VAT you have charged until you receive that money from your customers. There is less paperwork with the cash accounting system, but businesses who opt for it are not able to claim back pre-start-up VAT on business expenses. Accountants often advise registering for VAT and then changing to the cash accounting system later, particularly if pre-start-up expenses are considerable.

Developing a good relationship with your VAT inspector

Despite the fact that most businesses hate VAT, mainly because it adds to their paperwork, it can be a very useful tool for disciplining the small businessman or woman to keep accurate records. Also, the VAT system is fairly flexible and VAT inspectors are there to help and advise. You can, as discussed, change from the traditional to the cash accounting system, if you wish. You can do monthly or quarterly or even annual returns, depending upon which is more convenient for you. The VAT inspectorate will advise on how to deal with VAT on bad debts. De-registration, if you expect your sales to be below the VAT threshold of £50,000, is a simple procedure.

The main thing is to have a good relationship with your VAT inspector who will advise you willingly, from start-up to de-registration.

Insurance

Most people go through life with some life insurance, a household contents policy, mortgage insurance, buildings insurance and perhaps some health insurance.

You must inform your insurers if you become self-employed or start up a business from home. Some household contents policies may cover home computers, as these come into the sphere of home entertainment, but nothing more. You should in any case talk to your insurer about this. You will certainly need a special insurance to cover any business equipment, machinery, tools and other items necessary to your trade. You will not only need to insure them against theft, fire and any other hazard but also against breakdown and the consequential loss of business while they are being repaired or replaced. Currently, the high-street banks offer home contents policies which cover those conducting clerical/teleworking type businesses from home. There are also office equipment policies which cover certain items such as computers, faxes and answerphones. The average amount of cover would seem to be around £35,000. Some policies also cover business money (up to around £3,000) and stock and trade samples, up to a certain value, kept at home.

What you pay for your insurance depends very much upon what business you are engaged in. For example, furniture restoration involves the use and storage of flammable products, as does photography, if you develop your own photographs. Catering from home may be deemed by the insurer to be an increased risk of fire and so on. If you sell your wares in markets and fairs this will mean carrying large quantities of cash around and transporting your goods from location to location. You may be involved in mail order and need to insure your goods while in transit. You may rear animals or market garden crops and need a special veterinary or farming insurance.

Some off-the-shelf packages are available which cover particular trades but read the small print *very carefully* to make sure that every aspect of your operation is covered. Computer insurance, for example, is only of value if it covers the data (which may be your most valuable asset) as well as the hardware and software. If your house or workshop should burn down or be destroyed in a storm, you need to be able to rent somewhere else to work while repairs are being done, so this should be an integral part of your cover.

Some professional bodies and national associations have negotiated special insurance packages on behalf of their members. For example, a driving instructor may be able to get insurance cover that combines all his or her needs through the appropriate organisation.

Business insurances

A variety of business insurances can be purchased, depending upon the needs of your business or venture. They can be bought separately or put together in one package.

Engineering This insurance provides cover against electrical or mechanical breakdown for most machinery, including computers. By law, most items of plant such as boilers, lifts and lifting machinery must be inspected regularly by a qualified person but an insurer would probably require any pieces of machinery that you wished to insure to be inspected as well.

Money Money insurance is on an 'all risk' basis and covers cash, cheques, postage stamps and certain other negotiable documents. This type of insurance cover is particularly important if you have to move money around all the time, say from your home to craft fair to bank. Also, if your work, say in network marketing or collecting catalogue payments, means that you are going to be walking the streets carrying money, many policies include a compensation clause for you or your employee being assaulted during a theft of money.

Goods in transit This covers goods against loss or damage while in your vehicle or when sent by carrier. The sum insured may be a limit for each vehicle or for any one consignment. Very useful if you are trying to run a modest mail-order company.

Business interruption This compensates you financially for any loss or interruption to your business because of damage to your property.

Credit insurance Gives cover against the risk of debtors becoming insolvent and being unable to pay.

Book debts Cover against loss of money arising from accidental damage to or theft of books of account.

Frozen food Cover against loss of frozen food in deep-freeze units caused by breakdown or damage to the unit or failure of the electricity supply. Absolutely essential policy if you are running a catering business from home.

Glass Cover for the replacement of glass following malicious or accidental damage.

Legal expenses Policy that covers most business-related legal expenses from industrial tribunal hearings to high court actions.

Liability cover

The following areas of insurance cover are very important.

Employer's liability insurance   This is required by law if you employ anyone. It covers you if an employee should make a claim for injury, sickness or disability arising from their employment.

Public liability insurance   This is not compulsory but advisable. It covers you if a member of the public should suffer injury to himself or herself or his or her premises through your business and sues you – for example, you are a plumber and you flood someone's house or a member of the public visits your weaving studio, trips over an item left carelessly on the floor and breaks a leg. If you employ subcontractors you need to extend the cover to third-party public liability.

Product liability insurance   If you manufacture a product, even in a small way, you need to insure yourself against a lawsuit should a customer be injured by your product. If you think that what you manufacture could not possibly harm anyone, beware – there have been two cases in recent years that should be noted. One was of a handmade quilt manufacturer being sued because the wadding she bought in good faith, believing it to conform to the fire safety regulations, was in fact flammable and burst into flames, badly injuring a woman. The other case was of a woman who raised herbs from seed and sold the plants at craft fairs. However, she was either not aware of or neglected to mark those plants which had a poisonous or irritant effect and she was subsequently sued by a customer who developed painful skin rashes.

Professional indemnity insurance   This is of most interest to any business people such as freelance consultants or those running agencies, whose main job is to give advice. This insurance covers claims made against you if a client has incurred some financial loss due to your bad advice, fraud or negligence.

Motor vehicle liability   By law you must insure your legal liability for injury to others and damage to their property arising from the use of vehicles on the road – third-party insurance. Most business policies are comprehensive or third party, fire and theft. Comprehensive cover includes damage to your vehicle. The third party section of a commercial vehicle policy is usually limited up to £1 million. If you own more than five vehicles a fleet policy may be arranged.

Fidelity Guarantee or Bonding   This is insurance cover against loss of money or stock arising from dishonesty by your employees and is an insurance policy usually taken out by any company whose employees have to handle money on the company's behalf – for example, a salesman who takes payments from clients when he delivers stock for you.

Other insurances

Permanent health insurance   This is an insurance that provides you with some level of income if you are ill or have an accident. These policies usually pay out after an average of four weeks incapacity. Most policies set a maximum payout of three quarters of the insured's gross earnings for the previous 12 months.

Private medical insurance   is going to be of benefit if you cannot afford to be off work for a long time while waiting for treatment under the National Health Service. It is also extremely important to have a policy which pays you some income while you are incapacitated, as your earnings will be lower or non-existent for the period of illness or your business could collapse while you are ill. Private medical insurance premiums are always lower in group schemes, so it is worth checking with any relevant business, professional and trade associations to see if they have a scheme for members which works out cheaper.

Find out what is available

Most trade, business and professional bodies will tell you what insurances you need for your enterprise; trade magazines will probably carry articles about them. Alternatively, contact the Association of British Insurers★ or a reputable broker for comprehensive information.

Don't forget that pension

Once you become self-employed, your own retirement savings become crucial if you want to have more than just a state pension to exist on in your old age. You could consider a personal pension plan. However, *Which?* research has found some personal plans to be a poor deal. There are indications that better ones are coming on to the market. PEPs and ISAs are another option.

You may be one of the fortunate early retirees who has already collected a substantial pension and is just working from home to keep active. Others, however, should look to their old age and start providing now. When cash flow is a bit up and down, it is possible to subscribe to the 'recurring single premium' alternatives that accept occasional lump sums, often with far lower charges. You could also consider taking out a series of independent single premium plans as and when you can afford to.

Those who have let things slide should try to make up for lost time and make the maximum permitted contributions to personal pensions. They should also ask a pension company or adviser about using up previously unused allowances so that they can put as much money as possible into a pension fund.

It is also worth noting that the Inland Revenue recognises that cash may be short in the early years of working and increases the amount you are allowed to contribute to a pension scheme as you get older. It also reflects recognition that younger people give low priority to retirement planning and need to catch up later on.

Individual's age on 6 April	Max % of net relevant earnings	Cash limit during 1998–9 (£)
35 or under	17.5	15,330
36–45	20.0	17,520
46–50	25.0	21,900
51–55	30.0	26,280
56–60	35.0	30,660
61–74	40.0	35,040
75 and over	You can no longer contribute	

Chapter 7

Costing your work

This is an area where the experts advise you to go through specific formulae to arrive at the correct price to cover all your costs and make some money in addition. But, realistically, you first have to ask yourself: 'What price does my product or service have to be?' In other words, what you can charge for your product or services very much depends upon: what the customer is prepared to pay; and what the competition is charging for the same product or service. You may have little choice in this matter. For example, if you are a hairdresser, you know that your clients will only pay, say, £7.50 for a shampoo and set; if you run a driving school you know that your customers will only pay £20 maximum for a driving lesson.

So you have to start from the point where you know how much you will charge and why. The question is, can you make a profit? You then have to look at all your costs and see whether they are sufficiently low to enable your product/service to make you a profit. If not, can they be lowered? If they cannot, then you should rethink your undertaking.

It may be that you are not restricted in what you can charge for your product or service because it is something new, unique or rare and the customers may be prepared to pay highly for it.

Having decided which category applies to your business, you can then return to the conventional method of assessing your cost structure. It is an exercise which should be done very early on, before you start your venture. You will certainly need to do it if you are going to present a business plan to a lending institution, but it is advisable to do it anyway as you will not only arrive at a cost structure but also at an operating budget – that is to say, you will know how much you can afford to spend on certain items and whether your business, as you envisage it, will make a satisfactory profit.

Fixed costs

First assess your fixed costs. These are the costs that do not vary with the amount you produce – in other words, you have to pay them even if you produce nothing at all.

Write down a list, for example:

(Per year)	£
Any business rates[1] (say 12 × £50)	600
Electricity[2]	500
Telephone rental	200
Any loans	500
Insurances	500
Any equipment hire	500
Total	**£2,800**

[1] Don't forget that, even working from home, you could be liable to pay business rates.

[2] This should be the amount of extra electricity, on top of your household usage, which your business demands.

Variable costs

Next assess the costs to your business which fluctuate according to the amount you produce, for example, the materials you purchase to make your product, the packaging for your product, any seasonal labour that you might use.

This is a complex sum. Basically you have to assume a realistic figure that you will hope to produce and sell in your first year. Let us say that you are making soft toys and you plan to work alone for the first year. You buy your materials in a reasonable quantity from a wholesaler. You know that £60-worth of materials enables you to make 100 soft toys in one month, which you would sell at £10 each.

Make a list of your variable costs:

(Per year)	£
Materials (12 × £60)	720
Transport (running costs, petrol)	760
Postage (regular mail shots, etc.)	500
Telephone/fax calls	300
Extras (e.g. sewing machine repair)	100
	£2,380
Add your fixed costs	£2,800
Total	**£5,180**

Now we know that your total costs for one year will be £5,180. Divide that by the number of soft toys that can be made in one year:

i.e. $5,180 \div 1,200 = 4.32$

So each toy costs £4.32 to make and the resulting sale price of £10 should produce a healthy profit.

However, you must bear in mind that these figures are only very basic illustrations. Any accountant would advise you that you must build into your calculations hidden costs such as waste of materials, depreciation of equipment or any periods of illness when you cannot produce toys.

Other factors could influence your profit margin, for example:

- rise in petrol costs
- rise in postage costs
- rise in costs of materials
- competition forces down the market prices for your goods
- regular sales outlets lose interest in your product
- you need to make a large investment in equipment
- you need to expand and employ staff
- your customers force you to offer credit card facilities
- you acquire some bad debts
- you are forced to find money for legal fees.

Some of these can be built in at the planning stage. If you know, from the above calculations, what your basic profit margin will be, then you will have to allocate some of that hoped-for profit towards a contingency fund for those unexpected expenses. You will also have to engage in some costing exercises for possible future scenarios, such as expansion or diversification.

Diversification

Going back to our soft toy manufacturing operation, let us assume that you have your finger on the pulse of the market-place and you feel confident that you can produce soft toys that meet current trends, e.g. all the kids are mad about trolls, so you decide to manufacture trolls for a few months, in addition to your regular line. First you have to investigate the costs of the materials required to make the new product. Let us say that for six months you will allocate half your workload to the manufacture of trolls. Therefore your materials costs will be as follows:

6 × £60 (for your usual range)	£360
6 × £90 (for the new range)	£540
Total	**£900**

This alters your variable costs total by £180, bringing your total to £5,360. Divide this by your output of toys (1,200) and your new basic product cost is £4.47. So your profit margin has been eroded by 15p.

Whether to diversify or not is a 'Catch 22' situation. If you are still going it alone, then, on paper, all you are succeeding in doing is shaving 15p off your profit. But you may be in the position of not having any choice. If you do not offer what the market wants, it is eventually going to get tired of your limited range of soft toys and you will lose sales anyway. Often, diversification forces a business into the next phase of new calculations, which is expansion.

Expansion

If you employed someone to make a further 1,200 toys for you at, say, £6,000 per year (including tax and National Insurance), you could market them more aggressively. This in itself would necessitate expanding some of your other variable costs, such as transport and postage, as you would want to sell to more people and would presumably have more deliveries to make.

Let us redo the sums:

Fixed costs (remain the same for the moment)   £2,800
Variable costs:
Materials (as above but for two producers)

	£
12 × 60	720
12 × 90	1,080
Transport	1,000
Postage	800
Telephone/fax	500
Extras	200
Wages[1]	6,000
Total	**£13,100**

[1] Wages are regarded as a variable cost for the moment as the long-term situation may not work out.

So now we repeat the earlier sum. Divide the total running costs by the new number of toys (2,400) that can be produced in one year: $13,100 \div 2,400 = 5.46$

As you can see from this exercise, although you are actually selling a lot more toys, your profit margin has been eroded by £1.42.

If you do not really have any choice but to expand then you have several options open to you to get the profit margin up again.

- Trim your fixed costs, if possible. For example, you could: pay off any loans; get a cheaper loan; buy, not rent, telephone equipment (or any other equipment you may rent). Remember too that telephone equipment and service providers are in competition and that by shopping around you can get some very good deals.
- Trim your variable costs, if possible. For example, you could negotiate discounts with your suppliers for buying in bulk; subcontract or use self-employed workers who pay their own tax and NI; see if a delivery service would work out cheaper than using your own transport; negotiate special deals with postal services for all your mailshots. It is also worth comparing prices for utilities: by shopping around you could reduce your bills.

- Change your product yet again to one that can be manufactured at a lower cost.
- Find new ways of selling that allow you to sell at a higher price.
- Charge more for your products, if the market will allow. (For more on marketing see Chapter 8.)

As you can see, the whole business of costing is difficult but it has to be done. You have to know whether your product or service can compete in the market-place and make you money at the same time. If you are providing a service you have to cost by the hour and estimate how long it takes you to do a particular job. But, basically, you follow the same guidelines as above.

Of course, the figures above are optimistic. You know that you can comfortably make that number of toys in a year but will you be able to sell that number? What you need to work out next is your break-even point. In other words, how many toys will you have to sell in order to just cover your costs? The formula for this is as follows:

$$\frac{\text{Fixed costs}}{\text{Unit selling-price} - \text{variable costs per unit}} = \text{break-even point}$$

Taking the first set of figures in this chapter, for a toy manufacturer working alone, it would be as follows:

$$\frac{2{,}800}{£10 - £1.98} = 349$$

The fixed costs were £2,800. The unit selling price was £10. Dividing the variable costs (£2,380) by the number of toys to be made in a year (1,200) gave the figure of £1.98; 349 is the number of toys that have to be sold in a year in order to cover all the costs but not make any profit.

Pricing a service

Again, you are probably restricted by the current market rate for your service. Customers will pay no more and you may not be able to afford to undercut that.

Aside from *how much* you should charge there is the question of *how* you should charge. In other words, should you charge by the hour, the day, per project or ask for a retainer for an on-going job?

Charging by the hour

This can be the best way to charge for quick jobs, like word-processing, or work where you may be observed while you work, such as gardening, and the customer can see that a job really has taken several hours to complete.

Charging a daily rate

If a job is going to occupy one or two days of your time and you know you will not be able to offer a service to any other customers during this time, then charge a daily rate. It is reasonable for a daily rate to be slightly more than the combined hourly rate, to compensate for your time being monopolised by one job.

Charging per project

Hairdressers, masseurs, chiropodists and other such service providers charge per project. The public expect to pay a set fee per hairdo or pedicure rather than per hour. Consultants frequently charge per project, particularly if it is likely to be an unknown period of work, such as investigating a problem and preparing a report.

A retainer

If you are, say, a data processor, and one of your clients wants you to be constantly available to do their work but they cannot say exactly when that work will be ready, you would be in a situation to negotiate a retainer, i.e. a montly fee to keep you on standby. This fee reserves your availability; you would then be able to add your usual rates by the hour or the day. Being on standby does not prevent you from taking on work from other clients, but the client paying you the retainer must get priority when his or her work comes in.

The main breadwinner

The pricing calculations shown so far in this chapter really relate only to someone who is a second-income generator or has some other source of income besides their fledgling business.

If you are contemplating earning money from home and you are the person who pays all the bills, obviously that must be your starting point in all calculations. You need to earn enough money to pay all the bills. Your fixed costs are your domestic outgoings. If you are unable to cover those, you will not be able to survive, unless you can supplement your earnings with savings or state benefits, say.

There is no doubt that the businesses that survive those first tricky years are those that manage to keep costs down. Earning money from home is not a good idea if your overheads are so high that they are going to cripple your new business.

If your monthly outgoings are reasonable and you are, say, intending to take up an occupation that is truly home-based, and your spouse or partner intends to get a job and contribute some income while you look after the children's needs as well as your work – then perhaps you have a workable proposition.

Other factors in pricing

As we mentioned before, many external factors can contribute to changes in costs and, therefore, changes in your prices, so the costing/pricing exercise has to be repeated at frequent intervals throughout the life of your business. Here are some of the factors to be aware of at all times.

Interest rates

The interest rates on loans and mortgages can change. You may be lucky enough to have negotiated fixed rates for a couple of years and therefore those portions of your fixed costs will stay put for that period, but most people are subject to the rise and fall of interest rates.

Child care

Working at home and looking after your children may not be a workable proposition once you get a large quantity of orders/contracts/commissions. You may have to build in the extra cost of child care at some point which, if you have more than one child, can be considerable.

Other fixed costs

Insurance premiums will rise, as will the cost of telephone, electricity and gas, postage, petrol and so on. While insurance premiums may rise only once a year, items like petrol can become more expensive at any time and if your business is a heavy user of petrol this will obviously affect your prices.

Costs of material

Your suppliers will pass on any of their rising costs to you. You could also be in a position where your main supplier ceases trading and you have to find another source which is more expensive, or your particular materials may come from a part of the world which is suddenly ravaged by war, affecting supplies. You will then have to buy alternatives from other countries, which again may be more expensive.

Customer demand

Success does not always mean more profits. You could suddenly get a contract tomorrow to supply large amounts of your products, transforming you from a one-man/woman band into an employer overnight. Generating more goods means incurring more costs. The bulk-buying customer may also demand a discount, which you feel unable to refuse, and this obviously affects your general cost/price structure.

Customer demand, on the other hand, may peter out and you find that you have to diversify into other products or services, remarket them and incur a whole new set of costs, not necessarily greater but certainly different.

Time constraint

You may manufacture products that have a limited 'shelf-life' – seasonal goods that have to be sold before the relevant holiday (Christmas decorations), commemorative goods that celebrate particular anniversaries (Millennium mugs, for example), goods that cater to a passing children's fad (remember Cabbage Patch dolls?). Once the marketing opportunity is gone, the merchandise has to be sold at a greatly reduced price. The wastage of stock has to be built into the initial pricing decision if you are going into such a risky market.

Competition may get tougher

If your competitors start slashing their prices you could be in trouble unless you have allowed some margin for discount right from the beginning. This is why it is important before trading to work out in detail the profit you need to make on each unit (product or hour of service) in order to survive should any of the above external factors affect your business.

Budgeting

In order to decide how much income you would like to get, by costing your work and fixing a price, you need to draw up a budget for the forthcoming year. You have to look at your fixed costs and decide, before you commit them to tablets of stone (i.e. the business plan), whether they can be reduced at all. Remember to include any expenditure that you plan to make on machinery or equipment (unless that is covered under the all-purpose bank loan you intend to apply for). Business plans and financial forecasting are covered in Chapter 5.

With the variable costs, you have to ensure that your supply is the cheapest and/or the best; and the supply is safe and/or you have a back-up source of supply.

Cash flow

This is the most important part of your budgeting exercise because it shows money movements in and out of your account (see page 86). It will show when you will be paying bills each month or quarter, and when, it is to be hoped, money will be coming in from sales.

This is inextricably linked to your marketing strategy because how you choose to sell your goods determines the way in which your income is generated.

For example, you may make preserves. Half your stock is sold to farm shops – you bill them when you deliver the order and you give them 30 days in which to pay. So at the same intervals, but 30 days later, a certain amount of money will be coming into your account. The other half of your stock you sell every week at a market. Thus a certain amount of money is coming in every week.

One of the most dangerous things is to have too much stock, either in production or finished but in your home, or out with customers and no money due in for a long period. If you are a small producer you cannot afford to incur a lot of costs on materials, time and labour without an immediate return, or do business with customers who expect 90 days' credit before payment (see Chapter 11). It is better to produce and sell little and often at first.

Halfway through your first year your accountant or bank manager should be able to look at your books and compare them with your original budget. This will show whether your original estimates of work and sales were accurate. If they differ greatly, things have worked out better than expected or things are going wrong. This is then the time for analysis as to how you proceed for the rest of the year and beyond.

A formal quotation

Sometimes you may be asked to give a formal quote on price before the potential customer will place a definite order, particularly if you supply a service. A quotation is a legally binding document which could be used against you if you fail to keep to its terms, so you have to be absolutely clear in your written quotation exactly what you are offering for the price you are asking.

Make a realistic estimate first of how long the job will take you and what expenses if any you will incur in order to do the job. Let us say you are dressmaker who has been commissioned to make a wedding dress.

You will have discussed with the customer what type of dress she wants. Will it be straightforward or will she want hand embroidery on the bodice? Does she want one of your existing patterns or will you have to design something new just for her? Will she provide the material or will you? Will she come to you for fittings or will you have to go to her, thus incurring travel expenses?

Having sorted out the preliminary details you will then quote as follows:

• State exactly what service you are offering, e.g., designing the dress as well as making it.

- State who is providing materials – you or the customer. Emphasise that whatever arrangement is agreed, the material is of the customer's choice.
- How long you will take to do the job. (Put in the phrase 'unforeseen circumstances excepted'. That covers you if you are taken ill or some disaster occurs.)
- How many fittings you will require in order to complete the job.
- The price you are quoting for the job.
- How long that price will stand, i.e. how long the customer has to make up her mind before the price goes up.
- If it is relevant, reserve the right to alter the price during the course of the job should the cost of the basic materials go up, or the customer demands a change in the planned dress.
- Say whether the price is inclusive or exclusive of VAT, if that pertains to your business.
- Terms of payment, i.e. when the customer has to pay for the job. In this case, with a custom-made wedding dress, payments should be spread throughout the period of the job, with the first payment covering the complete cost of the materials so that you are not out of pocket should the customer disappear. It would be wise not to purchase the materials until this first payment has been made.
- Cancellation fee: in order to cover your time and effort you should state in a quotation that once an order is placed by the customer and the job has started it cannot be cancelled without some charges being incurred.
- Finally, ask for the customer's acceptance in writing. It may expedite matters if you include in your quotation an acceptance sheet which the customer just has to sign and return. It could just read as follows:

I have read the enclosed quotation and
I accept the terms and conditions
offered. I enclose the first payment
of £XXX
Signature
Date

Tendering

This is just another way of quoting for a job, except that you definitely know that you are competing for a job because several others will have been asked to tender. It is a common practice for, say, consultants or office service bureaux – any business that sells to other businesses.

None of the companies or individuals tendering a price will know what prices they are competing against. It is not always the lowest tender that is accepted, as other factors can have a bearing.

Never tender an impossibly low price for a job, no matter how desperate you are. You have to cover your costs at least. Never undervalue your time or expertise – it will only arouse suspicion in customers.

If, after the tendering process, you find that you did not get the job, ask why. If several companies tell you that your price was too high, then you can review your pricing structure and see whether you can resolve the problem. It may just be that you are competing against people who have a bigger profit margin than you, because of lower overheads, more resources and so on and can afford to quote lower prices. If this is the case, review your own service and see if you can offer a different, higher-value product.

Chapter 8

Marketing your work

Chapter 4 discussed market research and how to gather information to select the best markets for your work. You should have gained from this some pointers towards the best methods for selling to those markets. If, for example, your product or service is designed to sell to a specialist hobby market you may have discovered that the only way to reach that market is through targeted mailshots and by advertising in specialist publications. The product or service is then sold by mail order.

Alternatively, your research may have determined that your product or service is of most value to retailers and your marketing therefore has to be done on a one-to-one basis, visiting the retailers and persuading them to buy from you. This does not preclude a preliminary mailshot, of course, which can pave the way for you to follow up by telephone and make a sales appointment.

There are several methods of selling products and services from your home.

Putting a postcard in a shop window

This is a useful way of drawing attention to your service in a small community where shop-window postcards are frequently scanned. It is not recommended as the sole form of selling, however, if you really want to generate a decent volume of business.

Calling door to door with the products in hand

This may be suitable for agents or manufacturers of household products – in other words, where you have a small selection of reasonably light-weight products which might instantly appeal to a person at home during the day. (In today's society, unfortunately, many people don't want to answer the door to salespeople at night.) You need to have a car or van close at hand, so that you can keep topping up your hand-carried selection of goods. If someone decides to buy at the door they want to have the product instantly rather than place an order.

Delivering leaflets door to door (or car to car)

The leaflets advertising your service or product have to be eye-catching, the message has to be punchy and the contact information very clear. Leaflets stuck under windscreen wipers have a tendency to blow away and cause litter problems, or the drivers come back and immediately throw them away. If the local authority pick up several of your leaflets they might take action. Sometimes it is better to hand out leaflets at a strategic point – say the exit to a car park.

Delivering catalogues door to door (and returning to collect them)

This is double the work but you will eventually build up a round of regular customers who wish to order from your catalogue every month. However, the products contained in the catalogue have to be of limited life span, such as cosmetics or household cleaners – otherwise you will not generate regular sales.

Selling through agents or bureaux

If you use an agent you have to provide that person with back-up marketing material such as samples, leaflets or brochures, business cards and so on. Using an agent is a relationship of trust: you believe the person when he or she claims to have all the right contacts and can produce a certain volume of sales, while he or she trusts you to pay commission promptly and to meet the order deadlines and quantities. You should make it clear at the outset whether the agent is doing all your sales or whether you or a member of your family is also selling whenever possible. If the latter is the case, you need to

---

CASE HISTORY: Sally

Sally is a self-employed freelance writer and she gets all her work through
an agent. This agent finds Sally work writing magazine articles and books.
The agent takes a commission on all Sally's fees. The advantages for Sally
are that she does not have to spend time selling her skills as the agent has
a large network of contacts to call upon.

---

earmark an area for yourself and let the agent cover everywhere else.
You also need to discuss a pricing structure at the outset. You have
to build into your prices the agent's commission and also any delivery costs that may be incurred if the agent sells your product further
afield. You also need to be able to give the agent the latitude to offer
a discount for bulk orders and so on. All of this has to be built into
the pricing structure before marketing starts.

You may be offering a service as a subcontractor to various other
service organisations, for example you ring-bind reports typed by a
secretarial bureau or you hand-polish cars repaired or maintained
by a local garage. In this case you will do the initial marketing of
your service to the relevant organisations and they will continue to
market your service as one of theirs. You may have to agree that you
will not perform the same service for local competitors, which is
fair enough. However, you must reserve the right to shop around
and market your services elsewhere if the organisations do not provide you with enough work.

Selling to retailers

Quite often, craftworkers and artists find that shops will take their
work initially on a sale-or-return basis, and then place regular
orders. Having several retail outlets can provide a bedrock of regular income which leaves you free to sell in other ways that do not
compete with the retail outlets. Again, it is probably a question of
area. If you regularly sell paintings of scenes of Bournemouth
through a shop in that town, no one is going to mind if you sell
scenes of Brighton at a Brighton arts and crafts fair.

Selling through your own retail outlet

Many people take a stall at a craft fair or market as a first exercise in marketing. It has the advantage that you don't have to pay anyone else to sell for you but you probably have to pay for the stall space. It is of least advantage to a manufacturer because time taken to staff a stall for a few hours, plus the loading and unloading of wares, is time taken away from manufacturing. This type of marketing really works best for those who sell other people's products, for example they go to wholesale outlets and buy women's clothes to sell on at a profit.

Women's Institute (WI) co-operative markets are a good place to sell home-made, home-grown and hand-crafted goods. There are over 500 WI markets in England, Wales and the Channel Islands and they are usually held once a week in certain towns and villages. New producers are welcome and do not have to be WI members, but they do have to become shareholders in the County Market Society. WI markets are true co-operatives and everyone is expected to help run their market. The WI Country Markets* can supply a list of the local markets and information on how to become a shareholder and what is deemed to be suitable produce to sell.

Some craftworkers or caterers manufacture products all week and then sell them at fairs or markets at the weekend. This is fine if the sales generated justify you using up some of your free time, and if you have other sales outlets – it is very dispiriting to keep packing and unpacking the same products weekend after weekend and selling just a few items here and there.

Sending mailshots to targeted markets

This can be a good way of selling because you are targeting people you know are interested in your product or service (if you have got your research right, that is). If you are operating from home, be wary of inviting people to visit you – not just from the security aspect but also from the nuisance caused to neighbours by parking problems or unwanted traffic in what was previously a peaceful road. If you live on a farm with acres of space and you have made one of the barns into a furniture workshop, say, fair enough.

Selling by mail order requires careful planning and control. Timings, stock levels and credit control are crucial. You must also be very clear in any advertising about what your product or service is and what it is capable of doing. Under the various Trade Descriptions Acts and other legislation it is an offence to make a false or misleading statement about the goods or services.

Asking for payment in advance means that you must comply with the Mail Order Transactions (Information) Order 1976, which requires you to show your full name and address in any advertisement or mailshot. You may not use a PO Box number on its own.

The Advertising Standards Authority* in London can provide information on what you can or cannot say in a mail-order advertisement and lays down a format for accepted practice regarding times of despatch, refunds, supply of goods on approval and so on. Another source of information is the Direct Marketing Association.*

Direct mail

Direct mail, via the postal system, is still one of the best ways of selling but it has come under some scrutiny in recent years. If you hold personal information about people you must comply with the rules in the Data Protection Acts. You must register with the Data Protection Registrar.* You must make sure that the information you hold is accurate and obtained lawfully. The information must be accessible by the person to whom it relates but you must take steps to make sure that it is secure. You will need to get consent of the person to whom it relates to hold and process information about them.

The Data Protection Act 1998 comes into force in June 1999 and will replace the 1984 Act and anyone who holds personal information will have to comply with it.

The legislation applies to all businesses, large and small. Just because you hold information on a few people will not exempt you from registration and having to comply with the rules. Contact the Data Protection Registrar for information.

Post Office mailshots

If you want to target households in a particular area, say, several villages around the town where you live, it is possible to provide the

Post Office with enveloped mailshots and, for a fee, their postmen and women will deliver them with the morning mail. The fee is relatively modest and it is a good way of targeting certain sectors.

Advertising your product in newspapers, magazines and billboards

Advertising can be a hit-and-miss affair. It needs to be carefully targeted so that you do not pour money down the drain. A certain amount of experimentation is necessary and you have to analyse the results in order to gauge the return you are getting on your money. If you manufacture a product or provide a service to a specialist market you will have discovered, during your market research, those publications which cover that market. Several media directories (e.g. *Benn's Media* and *BRAD*) are published each year which list publications, their circulation and advertising rates. A good reference library should have them.

By comparing circulations and rates, you will be able to assess the ones that you think will give you the best response. You then need to study them and find what you think are the best positions for your advertisements. Perhaps you would like your advertisement to be opposite an article that relates to the sort of product or service you are offering? Perhaps you would like it to be under a special heading in the classified section? Negotiate with the advertising

---

CASE HISTORY: John

John strips and renovates pine furniture. He tried various forms of advertising – local papers, parish magazines, posters on noticeboards – none of which were really successful. He thought about his customers and realised that most of them were youngish couples who had just bought their first or second home and were looking for cheap but stylish pine furniture. He then hit upon the idea of advertising in all the estate agents' magazines and newspapers, and also paying for an advertisement to go on the back of all the house detail sheets that were sent out to interested buyers. This worked very well. He had reached the right market and demand for his products soared.

---

department of the publication. Take advantage of any special offers they may have. Read the section later in this chapter about 'free publicity'– it will have a bearing on your advertising policy.

It is generally true that just one advertisement will not give you a true picture of whether that medium works for you or not. Three consecutive advertisements are considered to be the normal 'try-out' period. By the end of that you will know whether to invest in more advertisements or try something else.

You could take some advice from an advertising agent. A reputable local company will be able to give you a preliminary report on where they think you might advertise to best effect and they will suggest a starting budget. Make sure that they understand from the beginning, however, the modest size of your overall budget, so that they won't waste time on grandiose plans.

You may find that one expensive (as far as you are concerned) little advertisement in a national magazine or newspaper generates so many sales that you are rushed off your feet filling orders. If this should happen, keep every name and address of the customers who ordered as a potential mailing list. The people who responded obviously liked your product or service and may be interested in anything else you have to offer. You can contact them directly in future.

CASE HISTORY: Sasha

Sasha buys plain T-shirts and appliqués beautiful designs on them to make them suitable for evening wear. She tried selling them to shops but the shops wanted her to cut her prices quite a lot in order for them to make a large profit. A friend suggested that she sell some T-shirts in her office canteen over a lunch period. Sasha did this and sold quite a lot of T-shirts. However, she could not afford the time to man a stall for several hours when she wanted to be making her products, so she approached a few large companies and asked the managing directors if she could set up an unmanned display in the canteen area where customers could fill in order forms and put them in a box, which she would collect later. She then fulfilled the orders, delivered them a week later and collected the monies outstanding. She sold just as many T-shirts but without losing any production time.

This applies to responses to any form of advertising. Keep those names and addresses on file. A mailing list of previous customers can be a great asset.

However, advertising or enclosing a mailshot in some national publications is not as simple as it seems. Because of past frauds and some companies going bust and leaving the customers without both money and goods, various organisations decided to set up the Mail Order Protection Schemes (MOPS) which are insurance plans that reimburse the readers if they should suffer at the hands of a mail-order company.

Each section of the media runs its own scheme. The National Newspapers Mail Order Protection Scheme covers national daily and weekend papers and their magazines. The Periodical Publishers Association covers most of the magazines in the UK and the Newspaper Society★ covers all the regional and local newspapers.

None of these organisations will allow you to advertise in any of their publications unless you have supplied the following information:

- the type of company you are operating
- your VAT registration number
- the registered address of the business and/or the operating address
- the number of staff employed
- financial information such as the amount of capital invested in the business, any loans outstanding, annual turnover, copy of the last annual accounts, type and extent of insurance cover.

The depth of detail demanded by certain publications can be quite daunting. Generally, the larger the circulation, the more stringent the entry rules for advertisers. The publication has to know if you can cope if you are swamped with orders from their readers. After all, it is not unknown for a single placing of an advert in a national newspaper to attract 30,000 orders.

Advertising on the Internet

Small businesses and one-person enterprises can use the World Wide Web facility on the Internet to advertise their services for a negligible amount of money. An advertisement in a national magazine can cost hundreds or even thousands of pounds, whereas a web site that can be seen by an equivalent number of people, takes about two weeks to design and costs perhaps £50 a month to maintain. If you subscribe to an Internet access provider then a free web site may be included in your monthly subscription. The other advantages of advertising on the Internet are that unlike an advertisement in a magazine or newspaper, a web site can be updated regularly and can maintain a record of the people who have 'visited' the site. You can use this to build up a profile of potential customers. You can also put high-quality images on your web site as well as text. You can make your site interactive by publishing a list of frequently asked questions (FAQs) about your product or service that interested parties can access.

The international nature of the World Wide Web makes it especially valuable if you want to sell a product all over the world to a specialised group. For example, a company manufacturing and selling daylight spectrum lamps for use by people suffering from Seasonal Affective Disorder would not wish to confine their marketing to the UK. By advertising on the Internet they can access most of the northern hemisphere and answer queries on their web site. Some estate agents advertise house-finding services on the Internet for business people moving to the UK.

CASE HISTORY: Ron

Ron owns a small video production company. He and his brother specialise in copying very old television programmes for the nostalgia market. They bought the video rights to various UK and American programmes from the 1950s and 1960s and they copy them for sale to the general public. The have several web sites under the names of the various programmes – for example, one site is *Robin Hood*, another is *The Milton Berle Show*. In the two years since Ron and his brother have advertised on the Internet they have built up a mailing list of over 22,000 TV nostalgia fans in the UK and North America and are beginning to attract attention from Australasia. Their customers also email them with suggestions for other programmes. Ron then investigates the programme with a view to acquiring the rights.

Delivering samples to an office or factory

Several network marketing book companies have adopted a sales technique of leaving sample books and order forms in offices and factories for the staff there to look at. The agent for the company returns a week later and collects the samples and the orders. The orders are then fulfilled and delivered to the workplace. If you are a small manufacturer, you could approach a local company or factory where the director will agree to you adopting this procedure and find a staff member there who is willing to take responsibility for your samples and order list. It is usual to offer this person some commission on sales or a free item from your range. One disadvantage to this method is that, if you cover several companies and factories, it will tie up a number of your samples.

Selling through a party scheme

This is a method of selling to an assembled group of customers at a 'party' where light refreshments – cheese and wine, say, or tea and biscuits – are provided. Many party scheme agents begin by asking a friend or relative to host the party in his or her home and to ask a group of friends or acquaintances round. The 'party' scheme works quite simply but relies on the host or hostess being able to gather a sufficiently large group of people; also, you or your agent has to be present to sell the product. Some companies, such as Dorling Kindersley and Ann Summers, have had success using this sales technique. You need to advertise, perhaps in the local newspaper, for party hosts and you need to vet the applications by visiting the intended party venue. It is not going to be very productive if the person lives in a very small house because you will not be able to display your products properly and there will not be enough people present to make it worthwhile. Also, the person hosting the party should have the sort of friends likely to be interested in and able to afford your wares. It's no good trying to sell hand-made silk quilts that cost £800 each to a group of young mothers on low incomes.

Getting orders by word of mouth

This works for some people, particularly those who produce commissioned work such as sculptures, tapestries or furniture. You may have a business such as upholstery or dressmaking where news of your abilities spreads from friend to friend and, before you know it, you cannot take on any more jobs. However, this is not a marketing strategy upon which anyone should base their future prospects. Even someone who has lots of clients from the start due to word of mouth should aim at some point to glean new clients through a different route.

Advertising in the *Yellow Pages*

This works very effectively for people who offer domestic services such as plumbing, bricklaying, carpet cleaning and so on. Whenever a job needs doing in the home, many people reach for the *Yellow Pages* and ring up a few numbers. You have to be prepared to visit the potential customer and give a free estimate, because that is what everyone else does. This can mean a high proportion of dead-ends but it could teach you something valuable about your marketing – perhaps you are overcharging or your timekeeping is not what it should be?

CASE HISTORY: Brian

Brian runs a fancy dress hire business from his home. He tried advertising in the local newspapers but it did not generate much business. He found that paying for a well-designed large display advertisement in the *Yellow Pages* was the best way to attract custom because of the nature of his business. Most people only require fancy dress about once a year and, when they do, they tend to turn to the *Yellow Pages* to find the nearest agency. The most eye-catching listings succeed.

Joining a professional body

This is a must for consultants of all kinds, because membership of a professional body means that your name and often your details are included in any membership lists or in any directories that are sent out to interested parties. It also means that you have access to the right market through the organisation's mailing list and newsletter or magazine.

Selling by telephone

This could mean selling your skills or your ideas (for example a consultant, journalist or writer who makes the initial sales pitch to a client or editor over the telephone) or getting an individual or a telesales bureau to sell your product over the phone.

Selling on radio or television

You might think that this is far too expensive for all except the multinational corporations, but that is not necessarily so. Local radio certainly is not out of the small business league and regional television sometimes has community advertising slots where reduced rates are offered to companies who want to reach a purely local audience. You could perhaps band together with, say, several other stand-holders at your forthcoming office services exhibition and purchase some air time to advertise the event.

Selling at special promotions

Some people sell their products or services only at exhibitions or conferences and find it a very successful way of marketing. If you have a product or service that appeals only to a niche market-place, where better to sell than at a gathering of people who are there only because of their interest in that very market-place?

When do you need help?

You can take advantage of marketing advice and help at any time, if you can afford it, but there are certain areas where specialist help is essential.

Selling your reputation

This is for those individuals who initially sell themselves purely on the strength of their CV – for example, consultants who put themselves forward for short- or long-term freelance appointments, either on their own initiative or through an agency. Making one CV stand out from all the others is sometimes the job of an expert, usually a recruitment consultant, who can advise on the arrangement of information and the presentation of a CV in order to achieve maximum effect. These people usually advertise in trade magazines or through the newsletters of the relevant institutes.

Selling your product or services abroad

This critical step requires as much help and advice from experts as you can muster. In the first instance contact your nearest Business Link Office★ if you live in England. In Scotland, contact Scottish Enterprise,★ and in Wales, Business Connect.★

Unless you are fluent in another language you will need the services of a translator because you cannot successfully market abroad in English. Even your letters of introduction to potential agents or customers should be translated into the relevant language. It does pay to use a professional such as a translation bureau rather than a friend of a friend who has an A-level in Spanish, say. You need a translator who is skilled in commercial and industrial language; you may even need someone who has a background in engineering, architecture or science. You must communicate effectively or you will only give a bad impression.

Selling ideas

This covers inventions, books, film or television scripts – anything that may need the help of a specialist agent (patent agent, author's agent and so on) or a lawyer.

CASE HISTORY: Maria

Maria makes wall tapestries and is particularly fond of including cats in her designs. After visiting a pedigree cat show, Maria decided to rent a stall at one of the shows and display her tapestries. The response from all the assembled cat lovers was so good that she sold more tapestries in one day than she had sold the previous month by other methods. She now concentrates solely on cat shows and has extended her product range to include cushions and bags with cat designs because customers indicated an interest.

CASE HISTORY: Vera

Vera makes embroidered silk blouses. A Spanish friend told her that she thought her blouses would be very popular in Spain. Vera went to a Business Link Export Development Counsellor for advice. The Counsellor provided her with a lot of market information which helped her pinpoint likely buyers and gave her the opportunity to exhibit at a British fashion trade show in Barcelona. From that trade show she got several contracts to supply department stores throughout Spain which she now does via a distribution agent in Madrid.

Any invention which you feel is totally new (it could be a household object or a board game) should be patented, in order to prevent exploitation of the same idea by others. The procedure for obtaining a patent is fairly complicated but there are patent agents who will deal with the whole procedure for a fee and advise on all aspects of patenting or other forms of protection of manufactured goods. Patent agents can be found listed in *Yellow Pages*. Also the Chartered Institute of Patent Agents★ should be able to advise you on which agents specialise in certain subjects. A patent agent will not help you sell your invention but he or she may be able to point you in the right direction through some useful contacts.

Authors' and scriptwriters' agents are often choosy about whom they take on their books. *The Writers' and Artists' Yearbook* and *The Writer's Market* are two publications which list all the agents and their specific areas of interest. Agents try to sell the writer's work and, if successful, take a commission on the sale, usually between 10 and 25 per cent. You can but persevere and hope that your track record or new work proves attractive enough for an agent to take you on.

Free or assisted marketing advice

All the organisations mentioned in Chapter 5 will assist in some way with the marketing process, either financially or by giving free consultancy time.

Anyone considering purchasing a franchise should, of course, find that training in marketing techniques and back-up material is included in the purchase price.

Smallholders, market gardeners, and those engaged in animal husbandry and rural or tourist industry activities may qualify for free advice and/or financial assistance from the Ministry of Agriculture, Fisheries and Food (MAFF),★ ADAS (The Food, Farming, Land & Leisure Consultancy),★ Food from Britain,★ the National Farmers' Union,★ the Rural Development Commission★ and the Regional Tourist Boards.★

Arts and Crafts are supported by their respective Councils in the form of either grants or loans for marketing (particularly in Scotland and Wales and areas of high unemployment) and they also have specialist consultants who will advise on marketing strategies.

Exporters fare particularly well. The Export Market Research Scheme (EMRS)★ provides professional advice on all aspects of international market research for companies with between 5 and 500 employees. Small companies may be eligible for a grant up to 50% of the agreed costs of approved marketing research projects.

For young business owner-managers, the Livewire★ Export Challenge (supported by Shell UK Ltd and Bass plc) provides specialist advice and training and an opportunity to undertake a market research visit to mainland Europe.

Plenty of free help and advice is on offer but it is best to do some research first so that you can pick the appropriate body that has an interest in your particular line of work. (This subject is covered in detail in Chapter 5.)

Using marketing professionals

This can be very expensive but it may be that you feel you could afford a one-off fee to pay a professional marketing company to look at your business and come up with a plan of action – ways in which you should tackle the whole business of marketing – which you could then use as a blueprint for all your future activities. Professionals may have some suggestions and contacts which you would not otherwise think of or stumble across. Don't be intimidated by the fact that a marketing company probably deals with accounts worth millions of pounds. If they are a good marketing company they will spot your potential as a future customer.

Low-cost ways of promoting sales

Now we come to the area of public relations, which you can conduct yourself very effectively. The aim of PR is to keep your name and product or service in front of the public as much as possible. You do not even have to be self-employed to do this – lots of agents, selling on behalf of others, become involved in self-promotion as part of their marketing strategy. There are various cost-effective ways to do this.

Sending out press releases

Compile a list of all the relevant media. These could be just local radio, newspapers, TV and magazines or might include the trade or hobby press. A press release is just a simple story – no more than one page – about something your business has achieved: a new product or service, an expansion, or some other event in which you are involved. If a photograph is relevant, send that too. You would be surprised to know how often local newspapers print small stories about local business people just to fill space in a 'slow news' week!

Some ideas for press releases might be as follows:

• You make soft toys and you have just sold your thousandth teddy bear.
• You make patchwork quilts and you have just had your first overseas order.

- You run a driving school and you have just taught someone famous to drive.
- You make children's clothes and you are donating some of them to the Romanian orphanages.
- You grow speciality plants and you are going to be featured on a TV gardening programme.

And so on – the ideas are endless. Some happen naturally, others you can create. Once you have trained yourself to think in public relations terms the ideas for continued promotions and the subsequent press releases will come thick and fast.

Writing articles

If you are an expert on a particular subject related to your occupation, write articles about it for the trade or hobby press. Many consultants build their reputations through writing authoritative articles in management and industry magazines. Copies of these articles can be included in any sales literature sent out to potential customers. Insist that you are properly credited at the end of the article, for example 'Mary Johnson runs a company from her home in Leicester called The Flower Tub' or 'David Smith is a freelance consultant engineer based in Harrow'. It is even better if you can get the magazine to include your phone number as well – after all, you probably will not be paid much for the article, if at all.

Giving talks and lectures

Get yourself on to the lecture circuits. This may be through the Women's Institute, Townswomen's Guild or some other organisation that is always looking for speakers on crafts, leisure pursuits, cookery or similar topics. Sports clubs are another outlet for after-dinner speakers (you must be able to inject a great deal of humour into your presentation!). Professional institutes and business organisations such as chambers of commerce are always looking for interesting speakers on business-related topics, as are Rotary Clubs and Round Tables.

The object is to give your talk and display your wares or sales literature at the same time, or hand around business cards.

CASE HISTORY: Elizabeth

Elizabeth grows herbs and sells them for culinary and cosmetic purposes and as plants. She advertises in one or two gardening magazines and gets a steady flow of orders for plants and seeds through those. After she started writing articles about the uses of herbs in cookery and catering magazines she began to get orders from restaurants for fresh herbs. Within just a year she was mailing a modest catalogue and price list to over 1,000 large restaurants in the UK and is now gradually building up a regular clientele.

Running workshops

This is an effective way to boost sales. If you grow flowers and dry them for sale to flower arrangers and florists, you could also run flower-arranging workshops and convert your pupils into customers at the same time. All you need to do is hire a local hall and charge your pupils a modest fee for the day to cover the hire, provision of refreshments and the advertising of the workshop. It should pay for itself, with the added bonus of extra custom at the end of it. You could also offer to run workshops during the summer at tourist attractions. Many 'living history' museums like to offer the general public an opportunity to see a craft at work. Local authorities are always on the lookout for people who can run workshops for children as part of their summer holiday activity programme. As long as you get some publicity out of it and it does not take you away from your main business too much, why not?

Giving demonstrations

Giving demonstrations is more or less the same idea as lectures or workshops. You demonstrate your skill – cake-decorating, sweet-making and so on, and promote your services or products at the same time.

Donating prizes to local competitions

Most local newspapers like to run competitions and are always looking for companies to donate prizes. You could do this in return

---

CASE HISTORY: Pamela

Pamela makes and decorates celebration cakes. She does sell to some bakery shops but she finds that she gets most of her orders from the regular cake-decorating demonstrations she gives to women's groups in the area. They are so impressed by her skill and the artistry of the finished cakes that they take her business cards and call her when they want a birthday, wedding or anniversary cake.

---

for some blurb about your company and perhaps a free advertisement. Insist that you receive all the entries to the competition because then you will have the benefit of the names and addresses of people who, although they did not win your product, might like to buy it if you write them an enticing letter.

You could donate prizes to raffles or draws held at local events but you get less benefit from that exercise unless the organisers are willing to give you free stand space in return.

Holding open days

If you are a market gardener, a smallholder, keep animals or have a craft workshop on your premises, you could hold regular open days and let members of the public in to see how you work. Give them all some promotional literature as they leave and, depending upon

---

CASE HISTORY: Sam

Sam and his family run a skip hire business from his home. The local village hall was desperately in need of funds so Sam conceived the idea of providing an adapted skip, with a thief-proof cover, into which all passers-by could put pennies. The skip, with his company name and phone number, sat in the car park of the village hall for three months, until it was full with pennies. It raised thousands of pounds for the hall and it gave Sam three months of press coverage in all the local media for very little cost.

---

your budget, a small free gift, and with luck they will buy from you in future. You could set up a special 'gift shop' for the day.

Staging publicity stunts

The world is your oyster here. You may specialise in hand-knitting jumpers so perhaps you could, in conjunction with the WI, organise a knitting marathon for charity, making sure that your name is featured prominently in any publicity. You may make sports clothing in a modest way and manage to persuade a sports personality to host an event for charity. You may have a lot of land around your house and could host a dog show and at the same time promote the hand-tooled leather dog collars you make.

Sending 'free' gifts

The gifts, of course, are not free to you. It is a common practice in business to send valued customers a gift at Christmas of, say, a calendar or a pen – something that carries your name and phone number on it. It is not a bad public relations ploy to copy, if you can make something small and cheap but charming that will encourage good customers to continue to buy from you.

Conclusion

The whole idea of marketing (and public relations) is that you should never rest on your laurels. You have to keep plugging away at your markets, carrying out research, anticipating any changes, developing new markets and continuing to impress your customers

---

CASE HISTORY: Christine

Christine hires out a bouncy castle to children's parties and other events. She dreamt up the idea of a bouncing marathon to raise money for a local hospital. The castle was set up inside a school hall and it was continually bounced upon for three weeks by schoolchildren and their parents, working on a rota system. It set a new record and got Christine lots of publicity.

CASE HISTORY: David

David hand-makes walking shoes and walked from Land's End to John O'Groats to prove the durability of his shoes. It generated publicity all over the country and even made national television.

with your efficiency, enthusiasm and determination. The image that you project, however small your operation, is an important part of the business of attracting custom.

Chapter 9

Buying equipment, support and skills

Equipment

Whatever occupation you are involved in, it is essential to have equipment that will enable you to function from home as efficiently and professionally as possible.

Telephone

Unless your work involves very few calls, you may want to consider having **separate lines** for domestic and business use. There will be a cost for a second line, for both the installation and the quarterly rental, but you will benefit from having a line free for clients' incoming calls, particularly if you attach the business line to an answering machine, and can escape from work calls if you choose to at weekends, say.

A plethora of special services, offers and discounts are now available to the private and business user. Some of these can prove exceptionally valuable to someone working from home. For example, one major company was offering a large range of business services, some of which are listed below:

Business mobile   For the price of one month's line rental, connection to voice mail and up to 10 hours (600 minutes) of talktime between the hours of 6 a.m. and 6.p.m. is also offered.

Voice mail   Works like an answerphone. Callers are greeted by your personal announcement and invited to leave a message. When you next use the phone you are alerted if there are any messages waiting for you.

Text messaging   You can send and receive text messages from the keypad of your mobile phone.

Call divert   Automatically diverts incoming calls to an alternative number, e.g. your mobile phone or a client's phone.

Call barring   Stops incoming calls for a specified period and can also set types of outgoing calls (e.g. premium rate or long distance) to be blocked to stop misuse.

Call waiting   A voice announcement tells incoming callers that you are on the phone and at the same time bleeps you to let you know that someone is waiting.

Calling line identity   An LCD display tells you the number of the person who is calling and you can choose whether to answer the phone or not.

Web commerce   The ability to use the Internet for the secure transaction of credit card payments as well as the fulfillment of orders.

ISDN   (*Integrated Services Digital Network*) lets you convert your single analogue line into two digital lines each capable of high-speed Internet connection. Most telephone companies now offer ISDN services for small business or home users. You would need to buy an ISDN card to connect your computer to the ISDN line. You can use one ISDN line for telephone calls, while using the other for Internet access or a fax machine; or you can use both lines for Internet access at twice the speed.

If you are a heavy telephone user, clients may get frustrated because you always seem to be engaged. It may be worth paying for a call waiting service. If someone is trying to ring you and you are engaged, you hear a bleep on the line. The caller will hear a ringing tone rather than an engaged one. By pressing a button you can put your first caller on hold while you deal with the second call, and then go back to the first call.

If you are not out but tend to be working most of the day in an outbuilding, say, the answer is to have a cordless telephone, which can be taken up to about 100 metres away from the house and still receive and send calls. It needs to be charged up at least overnight, and preferably more frequently.

Answering machine

Answering machines have transformed the lives of homeworkers because they enable customers to make contact with you even if you are out or working at something noisy or fiddly or that requires complete concentration. It also avoids the need for someone else to answer the phone on your behalf (such as a non-working spouse). If a customer gets no answer when ringing about a possible job for you, he or she may well ring the next number on the list and not bother to ring you back.

It may be important for you to be available at all times, in which case an answering machine is not the whole solution. If yours is a business where, say, you have several projects on the go and where you may be called upon to make decisions about any one of them at any time of the day, you need a system which enables you to be contactable at all times. Most answering machines have a **remote accessing device**, so that you can ring from another phone and listen to any messages that have been left. The disadvantage of this is that your customers will have to wait for you to return their calls.

A better way of accessing answerphone messages in case of urgency is to have a **pager**. The answering machine can be programmed to bleep you whenever a message has been left so that you can then get to the nearest phone. Several pagers now have display screens that show the telephone numbers of those people who have rung you or even a text message.

Of course, it is possible to get a great deal of technology in one package – **a combined answerphone and fax machine** is very useful, because these machines have the ability to take voice messages or switch to fax mode to receive faxes in your absence.

Many people still hate leaving messages on answering machines, so you might prefer to pay an **answering service**. Somebody you know who is confined at home, by a disability, say, might be prepared to work for you in this way, and some office bureaux offer such a service. You could have their telephone number printed on your business card (usually as a second number if the first number is not answered), and they will take any messages, assuring customers that you will ring back soon.

Alternatively, you could invest in a **mobile phone**. The telephone handsets themselves are relatively cheap but the charges for the line rental are still expensive. With a mobile, you do not necessarily have to print two numbers on your business card. At a fairly modest charge you could pay to take advantage of a call diversion service. This enables you, by programming your home telephone, to divert calls to your mobile in your absence. The advantage here is that keeping your mobile number secret from customers allows you some privacy at weekends if you want it; your answering machine can take messages, and your friends can ring you on the mobile.

Voice mail is also an option nowadays. All the telecom service providers offer this sort of service. Also, most have text message services like pagers.

Fax

If you will be doing a lot of business by fax you will need a separate line so that the fax can be left switched on permanently and not interfere with your ordinary telephone requirements. Otherwise, as mentioned above, you could choose an answerphone combined with a fax, which should be able to identify whether the incoming call is from a person or a fax. Most fax/answerphones can be set to ring a certain number of times so that if you are there you have a chance to answer a call before the other facilities come into play. One advantage of having a completely separate fax is that customers who want to send a fax but do not need to talk to you can do so without risking your answering the phone first.

A recent development is the fax card, which attaches to or slots into an ordinary computer, connecting the computer to a telephone line, thus enabling the user to receive or send documents as with a fax machine proper. The computer receives a document on screen, which then can be printed out. Fax cards are quite expensive and depend on the make of your computer. Some faxes enable you to take copies of documents, avoiding the need to go to a photocopying shop. (If you do lots of photocopying you will need to investigate hiring a proper copier.)

Faxes are among the appliances likely to be affected by the so-called millennium bug. This is because microprocessors dealing with date and time configuration may not be able to process the turn-of-the-century change or the ensuing leap year in 2000. To test whether your fax will experience problems, run the following check:

- Set the date to 31 December 1999 (i.e. 31-12-99)
- Set the time to 23:58 (or 11.58pm)
- Return to normal mode (so the clock starts to run)
- Record what happens when the time passes 'midnight' (what day/date does it show?).

To determine leap year compliance, first set the date to 28 February 2000 (i.e. 28-2-00) and proceed as above. If problems emerge you should consult the manufacturer, but note that if you bought the fax over six years ago your contractual rights have ceased (unless Scottish law applies, in which case you have five years from the discovery of the defect to take action).

Computer

Whether you intend to run a home office or are primarily a craft-worker or manufacturer, a computer could help streamline your business and assist with tasks ranging from basic accounting to producing state-of-the-art stationery and making sophisticated financial forecasts using spreadsheets. You can of course get by with a basic typewriter and a filing cabinet, but if your occupation involves any written reports, estimates, quotations or articles – anything that might need amending or updating, or any document that needs to be sent to several people – a computer could be a wise investment.

First, assess your needs carefully. If you have under £500 to spend and your existing system works well, you may be fine as you are. It is worth calculating how much time you waste on activities that add nothing to the value of the business, and balancing this against the time and cost of installing a computer. This is likely to total between £1,500 and £2,500 when additional expenses such as a printer, software, a maintenance contract and training are taken into account.

If you decide to buy, the key is to purchase the right **software** (the tools or programs which run on the computer) before choosing the computer itself and peripherals – the **hardware**. Think carefully about what you want your computer to do and the types of applications that will suit your requirements. If you want help with the accounts, for example, you can buy specialised software packages to help you deal with your finances. General-purpose business packages or 'office suites' include a word processor, a spreadsheet, a database, a business presentation package and extras such as a personal information manager. They provide a framework in which to work but must be tailored to your needs before you can use them – for example, you must create new templates for different types of spreadsheet. Before committing yourself, try to see software which interests you in operation. Don't be fooled into thinking that you need all kinds of elaborate applications if you will never use them. If you just want to write letters, a basic word processor should suffice.

Take advice from friends and computer magazines and do not be swayed by salespeople pushing the latest software package (this could prove an unwise investment if the product has not been sufficiently road-tested) or the fastest computer. Depending on your level of knowledge, you might want to go on an introductory course or use a consultant – an expensive option but worthwhile provided her or she understands your requirements.

Today it is possible to transform any enterprise with hi-tech hardware and state-of-the-art software. Below we list some of the possibilities:

Book-keeping   Programs to produce end-of-year accounts and automate VAT calculations, plus invoice- and cheque-printing systems.

Communications   With the aid of a modem, your computer can dial telephone numbers for you and send and receive faxes.

Computer-aided design (CAD)   Software for visualising two- and three-dimensional objects. Drawings are viewed on screen from any angle and easily altered.

Electronic banking   Statements can be sent direct to your computer, bills paid and money transferred at any time of day or night.

Image manipulation   Used by artists and graphic designers, this offers special effects not achievable by other means – such as 'morphing'.

Internet   Offers email, which enables messages to be sent from computer to computer almost instantaneously with attachments of images, sounds and other information, and the World Wide Web, a research resource and tool for businesses to promote their services internationally. You need a telephone line, modem and subscription to an Internet service.

Networking   Computers in a small office can be connected so that they share information and extras such as printers and scanners.

Presentation   Presentation applications offer libraries of graphics and symbols, including animation features, music and sound clips. Desktop publishing makes possible professional-quality stationery.
Personal organiser   Electronic organisers store all your vital information, can interlink subjects – e.g. people and projects – and remind you to keep appointments.
Specialist applications   Computer assistance with specific professional applications – for example, programs interface with sewing and knitting machines to design patterns, create embroideries and adapt garments.
Spreadsheets   Ideal for speculative calculations and profit management; information can be presented in tabular form and graphically.
Stock control   Databases can keep track of information and pick out trends and details.

Once you have purchased your computer there are several safeguards to remember:

- Keep the computer purely for business. Do not allow other members of the family to play games on it or to introduce other software that might contain a computer virus – it could wipe out your business records.
- Buy new disks that are marked 'guaranteed virus-free', and invest in virus-checking software if your computer does not already have this built into the system. Every time you receive a disk from a client, say, you need to virus-check it before accessing it.
- Regularly copy all the material stored on your computer on to back-up disks so that in the event of fire or theft you can retrieve the information. Remember, it is not your computer that is indispensable to your business but your data – you can replace your computer straight away.
- Keep a set of paper records, filed in a different part of the house. You will anyway have to make copies of all your accounts materials in order to send them to the Inland Revenue or VAT inspector.

The date change from 31 December 1999 to 1 January 2000 may cause some computers to stop functioning owing to microprocessors not being able to cope with the date change (known as the 'Millennium bug' or 'Y2K' problem). This is more likely to affect older computers. If you are thinking of getting a new computer, try to establish that it will not develop problems before buying. To find out whether your computer is Y2K compliant, contact the manufacturer giving details of model number, BIOS version and operating system and request confirmation of the computer's reliability. Remember that even if your computer is fine, software programs that rely on dates – such as spreadsheets, databases and accounting packages – may not conform, particularly older versions. A number of software programs are now available to test and fix the Y2K problem on computers and software packages. The more thorough also check the clocks to ensure they are aware that 2000 is a leap year.

Other equipment

Your initial market research will determine what other equipment you would benefit from. What do your competitors use? What manufacturing techniques do they employ? Can you afford to copy them?

If you have industrial equipment that cuts, sews, planes, welds, shapes, saws or performs any function that could injure or kill, safeguards are vital. You must be able to lock it away when you are not using it, and you must make sure that no unauthorised person is able to operate it or allowed to stand near it when it is in use. If safety gear is appropriate you must have it handy and wear it whenever you use the machinery – face masks and eye protection for working with dusty materials or chemicals; eye protection when welding or using chain saws or powerful garden strimmers; protective gloves when handling caustic or sharp materials, and so on. Never be casual about it. Just because you are very experienced does not mean that you cannot make a mistake.

Have the equipment serviced regularly, particularly if a third party is involved – as in the case of a driving school car, for instance. If you are a homeworker working for someone else, call in your employer if you have any doubts about the machinery. If you suspect a fault, switch off and do not use it again until it has been thoroughly checked by a competent person. It is better to be safe than sorry.

Do not keep machinery that uses fuel, for example petrol-driven lawnmower or oxyacetylene equipment, in any part of the house, not even in a scullery or conservatory. And do not keep photographic film or video tapes on open shelves – they can burn very fast and give off toxic fumes. Keep them in a fireproof, damp-proof cupboard away from the house. Ask your local Fire Officer for advice.

Buying equipment

When it comes to choosing the best-value piece of equipment for your purposes do some research to enable you to shop around effectively. *Which?* magazine has published surveys on most kinds of domestic and office equipment, with test results on the level of performance you can expect for your money, and with recommendations for those items offering best value for money.

Specialist equipment may have been the subject of similar surveys by trade associations. It is worth enquiring whether the association relevant to your line of work has done tests on the type of equipment you intend to buy and can make recommendations.

Similarly, you can often find informative articles in trade magazines or papers. Industrial sewing machines, for example, might be covered in clothing industry magazines or manufacturing publications – it will pay you to look in both areas.

You could also go to an independent dealer who stocks most, if not all, of the makes of equipment that interest you. Go armed with a list of questions: you need to know exactly what you want from your piece of equipment so that the dealer will be able to make a positive recommendation.

What do you want to do with it?   How demanding are you going to be? Will you be using it all the time? In which case, does it have a powerful enough engine? An ordinary domestic lawnmower, for example, cannot cope with being used continuously for large areas of grass – the motor would burn out.

Do you need to carry it around with you?   If you are on the road a lot, do you need portable equipment? A mobile hairdresser will need equipment that can be loaded and unloaded easily, as will many others – caterers, masseurs, aromatherapists, beauticians and so on.

Do you need it to be flexible?   Do you need power tools, for example, to do the small intricate jobs as well as the big hefty ones? Do you need equipment that is battery-operated, so that you can use it anywhere?

Do you need something sophisticated or can it be simple? Think carefully about what you need from your equipment. Do not be tempted to buy a state-of-the-art machine if you plan to put it to fairly basic use.

Does the price of the equipment vary from stockist to stockist? Do your cost comparisons before you buy. Look in shops and dealerships, browse through trade magazines, ask at trade associations. Are there any special deals on offer if you are a member of an association? Is the price cheaper at certain times of the year? Computers, for example, often get more expensive just before Christmas, because they have a domestic as well as a business application. Ask if there is a discount for cash. Some shops are prepared to forgo the percentage they would normally pay to a credit card company if you pay cash (not cheque).

Do you have to have accessories? Sometimes you cannot do without them for reasons of health and safety – for example, a face-guard for use with a chainsaw. Other accessories may not be important or you may be able to get them cheaper elsewhere. If a piece of equipment is being offered with the accessories as a 'free' gift, check that the price of the package really is a bargain and that you cannot in fact get it cheaper elsewhere.

Do you need to upgrade your machinery regularly? Hiring may also be a better option to avoid built-in obsolescence (see below). The older the equipment the more difficult it is to get spare parts. (You certainly do not want to buy second-hand in this case.)

Do you have to buy, or would you be better hiring? Hiring can also be a better option if you need a piece of equipment for a short time only (perhaps at a trade fair or exhibition being held at the other end of the country) or you want to experiment by offering another product or service but are not willing to commit yourself to buying machinery until you know there is a demand. If there is any element of risk in your situation, you may prefer to start off your business by hiring rather than taking out a loan and buying.

What about back-up? If your equipment fails and will take several days to be repaired, where can you get something to tide you over? Arm yourself with that information before you buy. If you do buy, particularly if it is an expensive piece of equipment, can you get a temporary replacement clause built into the sales contract, or will you have to replace the item through your insurance policy?

Do you need an extended guarantee? Nowadays, most equipment carries with it the option of paying for an extended guarantee period. The equipment will carry a free guarantee for, say, up to one year, and you have the option of taking out an insurance which covers you for three or five years, or whatever the manufacturer feels is appropriate. However, study the small print of the contract very carefully. Some extended guarantees do not cover 'wear and tear' and some exclude business use. One alternative to these guarantees would be to take out a maintenance contract with a company which, for an annual fee, will cover you for regular services and repairs. Another option is to hire your equipment, in which case it should automatically be covered for any repairs or replacements.

Insurance

Insure all your important equipment against damage or theft. You will need to replace it quickly to keep your business going.

Your rights as a purchaser

Cancellation

Some goods are not available instantly and have to be ordered from the manufacturer. The salesperson may tell you there is, say, a four-to six-week delivery period. If you accept this and sign an agreement, you are not entitled to cancel the order unless the goods have still not arrived after the agreed time, and you have given the seller a deadline, in writing, before cancellation, for example, 'I am informing you that if my automatic wine-corking machine is not delivered by the end of next week, I am cancelling the order.'

Delivery

Under the law it is the buyer's responsibility to collect goods unless the seller has agreed to deliver them. Mostly, companies will offer to deliver but for a charge. It makes no difference under the law whether you are disabled or elderly – the seller has no legal obligation to deliver unless you are buying a piece of equipment that, for safety reasons, has to be professionally installed or built on site. The legal obligation lies with whoever installs the equipment, should a death or injury arise from faulty installation of the equipment. Bear that in mind if you decide to do it yourself. Also, there are certain pieces of equipment that have to be regularly inspected in order to comply with regulations – such as high-pressure water heaters or special electrical installations.

Return of goods

You have to have reasonable cause to return goods that you have bought, which is to say that they have to be faulty, unfit for their purpose or not comply with their description. You cannot simply return a van because you have decided you do not like the colour after all, for example.

Hiring equipment

Read the rental agreement carefully. Points to look out for are:

Insurance

Most rental companies will expect you to take out insurance to cover the cost of the goods if they are damaged or stolen.

Minimum hire period

You may want to hire something for only a week while you are at a trade fair, but the hire company may have a policy of a minimum one-month hire period.

Location of equipment

A hire company has the right to insist that the equipment is kept at one particular place, such as the home or office. The contract may stipulate that you cannot travel with it, or that you cannot keep it in a shed in your garden.

Early termination of agreement

You cannot normally be made to sign up for longer than eighteen months at a time without a chance to end the agreement by giving 'reasonable notice' as specified in your agreement. Check that the agreement you are entering into allows for an early termination. If your business folds you do not want to be bound to hiring a piece of equipment you no longer need.

Service or maintenance clause

You want to be assured that in the event of breakdown or other problems the hire company will repair or replace the equipment as fast as possible at no cost.

Your obligations

You must take good care of the equipment you are hiring: you will be liable for its cost if it is damaged through your negligence. You must also pay your rental instalments when agreed or the hire company may be entitled to repossess the goods. However, note that if you fail to pay only one instalment, the hire company can only repossess the article if your agreement says so.

The hire company's obligations

The company is obliged to supply you with goods which are suitable for the purpose for which they are wanted, and are in a safe, working condition. It is required to make some arrangements for service or maintenance, either by doing it or providing the name of a company with whom it has a special arrangement. The company must replace any equipment that cannot be repaired, unless that situation has arisen through your negligence. Again, **always check the terms and conditions of any agreements before you sign them**, so that you are aware of exactly where obligations lie. Some companies require the hirer to pay for an insurance which covers the piece of equipment in the event of damage.

Hire purchasing equipment

This is a form of hiring but the ultimate aim is to purchase the goods outright. The usual structure of the contract is that the customer pays an initial deposit and then further regular instalments (which cover the purchase price) plus an interest charge on the overall amount. The final payment is deemed in the contract to be an amount which is not part of the hire but is an 'option to buy'.

Frequently, a hire purchase agreement is between a customer and a finance company, not the trader who is selling the goods. The finance company, in effect, owns the goods that are hire purchased and therefore is the party that must be contacted and held liable for any defect in the goods.

The seller's obligations

The seller is obliged to give the goods to you in sound condition as soon as you have paid the deposit. The seller is also obliged to allow you to have full use of the goods without interference, provided all agreed payments are forthcoming.

The seller is also required by law to be a complete owner of the goods being offered for hire.

Your obligations

You must look after the goods for the period of the hire purchase agreement. (After the final payment you can do what you like with them.)

You must keep them insured for their full value against damage, loss, theft and so on, and you must not sell, pawn or hire out the goods while they are still subject to the hire purchase agreement.

If difficulties arise

The law recognises three distinct ways of backing out of a hire purchase agreement.

Cancellation　　This means cancelling an agreement before it starts. If you sign an agreement in your own home rather than at a place of business and if the agreement is a consumer credit agreement, there is a statutory five-day 'cooling-off' period during which you may cancel the agreement; the seller has to return any deposit or part-exchange goods (or a part-exchange allowance in cash). This is designed to protect people from succumbing to high-pressure sales techniques used on them at home.

There is no 'cooling-off' period if you sign an agreement at the seller's business premises, so you cannot cancel. You can usually cancel if you have agreed to buy something by mail order. The seller will usually specify a period during which the product must be returned if a refund and cancellation are required. The 'pressure to buy' is deemed by law to be much less in such circumstances.

Withdrawal　　The ability to withdraw from an agreement depends on whether or not the seller has signed the agreement. If you have signed an agreement at a seller's business premises, you cannot cancel. However, if the seller has not completed his or her side of the contract, that is to say signed the agreement undertaking to fulfil his or her obligations as a hire purchaser and given you a copy, you are able to withdraw from the agreement by notifying the seller as quickly as possible in writing. But, be warned, the seller is deemed to have completed the deal upon posting his or her copy of the agreement, so if your written withdrawal and the signed contract cross in the post, the chances are you did not get in quickly enough and you will have lost the chance to withdraw.

If your withdrawal is successful, you should be entitled to an immediate refund of any deposit paid or goods taken in part-exchange.

Termination If you have difficulty keeping up with the payments you can terminate a hire purchase agreement, usually after a certain point in the life of the contract. Most agreements stipulate that the buyer has to pay at least half the total cost of the goods plus any extras that may have been incurred such as insurance, installation charges or delivery. Once the goods have been returned there is no more to pay.

If you owe money to the seller when you decide to terminate, you will be liable to pay any outstanding amounts up to the date of official termination.

What the seller can do

If you have not kept up the payments or returned the goods, or unlawfully sold the goods to someone else, the seller is able to take certain action.

First, the seller must send you a default notice which details why you are in breach of the agreement and what the seller wants to do about it, that is, whether you must pay the money you owe and/or return the goods, or pay compensation for the value of the goods.

You have seven days in which to respond to the default notice. If you do not respond the seller has the right to ask your permission to repossess any of his or her goods that are on your property. If you do not give him or her that permission the seller can get a court order to repossess.

If there are no goods to repossess, the seller can take court action to recover whatever monies are owed in respect of hire purchase and in lieu of the goods that have gone missing.

If you agree to hand back the goods without the seller having to get a court order to repossess, you will also have to finish paying one-half of the total hire purchase price.

Financial help with equipment

Some of the organisations mentioned in Chapter 5 may be able to offer loans or grants towards the purchase of essential equipment. It is always worth checking to see what the current position is. Some of the Homeworking Units, the West Yorkshire one, for example, will loan certain equipment to homeworkers – equipment that contributes to the health and safety of workers, such as adjustable chairs and lamps, smoke alarms, circuit breakers, first aid kits, scissors, aprons and sticky tape dispensers.

Getting support

You need the right equipment to help you work successfully from home but you also need the right information and specialist advice to help you to function. This kind of support helps you to make the best decisions for every aspect of your new business.

All the organisations mentioned in Chapter 5 can offer lone entrepreneurs and small businesses the additional skills and support they need for growth. The Training and Enterprise Councils (TECs)★ and Business Links particularly help you to identify your business needs and a number of their support services are provided either free of charge or at a very modest cost. (LECs, Scottish Enterprise★ and Business Connect★ in Wales).

These organisations aim to provide contacts to help overcome the problem which faces many individuals who work from home – isolation. One solution to isolation is to 'network'. Networking is the process of making business contacts, building up a network of people who will become your support services, your customers, perhaps even your partners and friends.

Some of the many sources of support are outlined below, but first you need to assess the areas in which you may need support.

Financial

As discussed earlier in the book, unless you are a qualified accountant yourself, it is advisable to get someone to organise your account books, advise on credit control, raising finance, tax and other matters. However, if you are starting small, you may need no more than some advice from your local Business Link, bank manager, Inland Revenue and Contributions Agency. On the other hand, if you are starting an ambitious project it would be prudent to use the services of a professional accountant from the beginning. Whatever size your enterprise, it is advisable to get an accountant to audit your accounts once a year for tax purposes.

If you have no experience of accounting at all, you may need the support of a book-keeper who will come in, say, once a week to put your books in order, enter all receipts, sales, expenses and so on.

At one time, before the high-street banks cut back on their staff, the first port of call would have been your bank manager. However, a manager now often has two or three branches to oversee and is rarely available to give that sort of advice. Some banks have trained a member of staff to be a 'small business adviser' but his or her time and experience is sometimes limited.

Your local Enterprise Agency,★ TEC or Business Link can put you in touch with qualified people and also offer help with training in basic book-keeping skills, as well as supplying you with literature produced by the government and specifically aimed at helping small businesses organise and maintain their accounts.

Legal

Many people tend to retain a solicitor only when there is trouble but a solicitor can help a lone entrepreneur in many ways. Many solicitors publish a scale of charges for uncomplicated jobs, such as writing letters to bad debtors or drawing up a contract of employment. It is worth discussing your future needs with a few local solicitors to see what charges you might incur.

For basic advice on contracts or consumer matters you can contact your local Citizens Advice Bureau or join the *Which?* Legal Service at Consumers' Association.★ For a modest quarterly fee you can phone the Legal Service whenever you have a consumer problem. If your problem escalates into one which requires further action, the *Which?* lawyers will quote a fixed fee between £50 and £300 to help you sort out the problem.

You may find yourself in a situation where you have to recover a bad debt through the Small Claims Court, in which case you will not need legal advice as the system is specifically tailored to meet the needs of people who are not familiar with legal procedures. The forms have accompanying notes and the procedure, once you attend the court, is explained in simple language.

Your local authority will be able to offer advice on rules and regulations that may apply to your setting up in business. Local authority literature covers a wide range of occupations and explains the relevant government and EU regulations.

Most trade and professional associations have legal departments which give advice to members. They may hold seminars on legal problems which often beset their particular industry. General professional bodies, such as the Institute of Directors (IOD)★ or the Institute of Management,★ offer free legal advice to members on any problems relating to the running of a business. The IOD, in particular, publishes lots of material and runs frequent seminars on the legal liability of company directors, which apply to any company whether it comprises two people or two hundred.

Marketing

You can find support for your marketing activities from all sorts of sources, as described in Chapter 4. You can use published market research in libraries or on the Internet.

Employing marketing consultants can cost a great deal of money and readers of this book should turn to the organisations mentioned in Chapter 5 first to see if they can get such advice free or grant-aided. Local advertising agencies, however, may be within your budget. Ring them up to see if they will give a free initial consultation to look at your particular marketing problems and suggest a tentative plan of action, outlining their costs should you wish to proceed.

Selling direct to the public is governed by a code of good practice which was drawn up by the Direct Selling Association★ in collaboration with the Office of Fair Trading. The Direct Selling Association can offer advice on all aspects from door-to-door selling to party plans.

You should also contact your local Trading Standards Office, who will be able to offer you free advice on how you must sell your goods. They can also provide a wealth of literature regarding the current rules and regulations for labelling, safety requirements, trade descriptions and so on. They willingly advise anyone who simply has a business idea and has not yet set up in business.

Mail order

The first place to go for advice is the Advertising Standards Authority.★ It lays down the British Code of Advertising Practice, with which all mail-order firms have to comply. If you intend to advertise your products through a newspaper or magazine you will have to get details of the Mail Order Protection Scheme (MOPS) run by the relevant publication.

On the practical side of mail order – forms of packaging, times and frequency of despatch and so on – both the Post Office and ParcelForce will gladly discuss with you your proposed venture and suggest ways and means of dealing with your despatch needs. So will any of the private security/courier firms such as Securicor, Group 4, DHL and others.

You may find that you need a few sessions with a specialised consultant in order to determine the best sources and types of packaging. Your local Business Link or Enterprise Agency should be able to help.

Export

An enormous amount of advice and support is available for the individual who feels that his or her product may do well in an overseas market.

If you are resident in England, your first port of call should be the Business Link Office.★ In Scotland contact Scottish Enterprise.★ If you live in Wales, contact Business Connect.★

The British Standards Institution★ gives technical advice to ensure that your products comply with the various overseas standards.

The Central Office of Information★ can offer advice and practical help in export publicity services to make your product better known overseas.

Most trade and business associations and Chambers of Commerce★ run export clubs or forums where potential or new exporters can network with experienced exporters and learn more about the procedures and pitfalls of exporting. Sometimes financial help is available in the form of subsidised overseas marketing trips or similar.

Most of the above-named organisations will be able to put you in touch with good commercial translators who will help you overcome the language barrier when starting to export to non-English-speaking countries. Also, if you intend to advertise abroad, you will need the advice of an advertising agency versed in the rules and regulations governing advertising in those countries. These regulations vary enormously and have to be strictly adhered to.

Other support

You will certainly need advice on what insurances you must have and what you can afford. An independent insurance broker is the best source of advice but do shop around – you can make quite a saving by looking at what is on offer before you actually buy. Remember to read the small print very carefully to ensure that you are getting cover for what you need and not duplicating cover you already have on another policy.

You may need help with technology, either because you do not have the right technology to do a particular job or your existing technology needs a good service back-up. TECs can help here by perhaps putting you in touch with a potential subcontractor who has the right technology to undertake a particular job on your behalf, or a local office services bureau might be able to offer the amount of support you need if a particular job has swamped you and you need help for just a short period. The place where you bought your equipment should be able to recommend a good service engineer or, if you bought it second-hand, you could ask for advice at your local Chamber of Commerce or trade association.

Last but by no means least, enlist the support of your family and friends. Apart from being extra pairs of hands when the workload piles up, they can also be excellent sources of information and fresh ideas. It is a common trap for the individual working from home to operate in a vacuum. Ideas become stale, problems get out of proportion, the ability to delegate disappears. Let others support you in whatever ways they can and you will find that you get greater enjoyment from your work.

Getting skills

You may be contemplating starting a career from home which requires you to learn a new skill from scratch, or you may feel that although you are already skilled in your field a formal qualification will inspire more confidence in your customers. Indeed, you may not be able to operate certain businesses – for example, a driving school – without formal qualifications. You may want to learn new skills to help you to diversify from the product or service range you are currently offering. Alternatively, you may be acquiring a new piece of equipment which demands a period of training to acquaint yourself fully with its finer points.

There are many places to go for the necessary training: Adult Education Institutes (evening or day classes), universities or colleges (for full-time courses) or correspondence courses (for diplomas in a wide variety of skills from accountancy to interior design). Other courses can be found by contacting the manufacturers of the equipment you want to buy or by visiting your local library, JobCentre or nearest Training Access Point (TAP). Training is discussed in detail in Chapter 2.

Again, many of the organisations mentioned in Chapter 5 offer support for training in certain skills and, sometimes, grants for the same. The Department for Education and Employment (DfEE) offers a Career Development Loan. The government helps people to pay for vocational training by arranging with some of the high-street banks to offer special loans. The government pays the interest due on the loan for the duration of the course and for up to one month afterwards. Then the borrower has to repay the loan, plus any further interest, in instalments. The borrower may train full-time or part-time, or use open learning. The loans are available for up to 80 per cent of the course fees and, in some cases, living expenses if you are on a full-time course.

To qualify you have to be over the age of 18 and not in receipt of any other support for training or education, and undertake to work in the UK or elsewhere in the European Union after the course is completed. The course has to be suitable for the work you want to do and last between one week and one year, and the loan has to be for between £300 and £5,000. Further information is available from your local JobCentre.

People who have been unemployed for more than 12 months may wish to opt for the Training For Work scheme. It is possible under this programme for an individual to receive training and financial support to assist their move into self-employment. Information is available through local JobCentres.

Some local TECs and LECs may provide financial support to start-up businesses.

All companies that are members of the British Franchise Association★ undertake to offer full training in the operation of their franchises. After all, it is entirely in the interest of the franchisor to ensure that the product or service continues to carry a good name by being operated by skilled people.

Training on specific pieces of equipment should be no problem, although it may not be a free service if it requires more than half a day's instruction. Many Adult Education Institutes are now running computer software courses where you can learn the intricacies of desktop publishing or get to grips with word-processing packages. The advantage of such courses is that they allow you to learn at a steady pace, perhaps before you invest in the relevant software. Many manufacturers now offer training videos, often free of charge, with each new purchase of equipment. Again, these are a good idea because they provide more insight than a manual and they can be played over and over again until you feel confident you know what you are doing.

If you are a craftworker who would like to add to your skills you can look in some of the art and crafts publications to see what courses are on offer or contact the Crafts Council,★ which publishes a huge, regularly updated list of courses throughout the country.

Chapter 10

Wading through the red tape

If you asked most owners of a small business what they feared the most about working for themselves they would probably say that it was having to deal with local government, central government and EU regulations – in other words 'red tape'.

Most businesses are subject to regulations. Below is a list of some of the Acts and regulations with which you may have to comply.

Acts of Parliament
- Animal Boarding Establishments Act 1963
- Trade Descriptions Act 1968/72
- Supply of Goods (Implied Terms) Act 1973
- Consumer Credit Act 1974
- Health and Safety at Work, etc. Act 1974
- Patents Act 1977
- Unfair Contract Terms Act 1977
- Sale of Goods Act 1979 (as amended)
- Local Government (Miscellaneous Provisions) Act 1982
- Supply of Goods and Services Act 1982
- Consumer Protection Act 1987
- Food Safety Act 1990
- Registered Homes (Amendment) Act 1991
- Data Protection Act 1998

Regulations
- Nightwear (Safety) Regulations 1985
- Furniture and Furnishings (Fire) (Safety) Regulations 1988 (as amended)
- Electricity At Work Regulations 1989

- Toys (Safety) Regulations 1989
- Town & Country Planning (Control of Advertisements) Regulations 1992
- Food Safety (General Food Hygiene) Regulations 1995

Other

- British Standards mark or European Approval mark
- Local authority planning regulations
- Local authority licences.

It can be dispiriting to someone who is simply developing a hobby into a business to find that once he or she stops selling to friends and starts selling to the general public, a tidal wave of regulation looms up.

It has been reported in the national press and other publications that one of the biggest problems encountered by many individuals is the fact that many of the newest regulations emanating from the EU are not specific enough and are open to wide interpretation by local and central government officials. This has resulted in many businesses being forced to close down because they have supposedly fallen foul of the regulations.

In 1994 the government passed the Deregulation and Contracting Out Act which gives businesses the right of appeal through a local magistrates' court while, at the same time, giving them the right to continue to operate until a decision is made.

Take advice

One of the best places to start is your local Trading Standards Office, which will have a Department of Regulatory Services (or similar title). Even if you just have a business idea at this stage, they will be able to advise you on what legislation will be applicable to your enterprise. They will provide you with the latest literature and tell you whether any new regulations are likely to come into force in the coming months. Most of the literature originates from the Department of Trade and Industry★ or, if the subject is food and produce, the Ministry of Agriculture, Fisheries and Food (MAFF).★

Women's Institute Country Markets,★ for example, give their potential stallholders leaflets explaining the legal requirements for different types of products, for example, that preserves have to be in clear glass jars of particular sizes; labelling has to be done in particular ways and must include the maker's full name and address; and so on.

Starting at the beginning

First, make sure that you are allowed to conduct your proposed business from your home. Check your lease or mortgage and your house insurance. If your proposed business is allowable, in that it is not noisy, hazardous, likely to cause offence to the neighbours or require alteration to a listed building in a conservation area, the chances are that you will be able to proceed.

If you are going to change the use of your premises (into a treatment room, tea room, shop and so on), alter the shape (build a workshop over your garage or similar) or the appearance (install a large shop window in the front or put a sign on the door) you will have to seek planning permission. Most local authorities provide leaflets which explain the application procedure for planning permission.

A number of businesses cannot operate without a licence. The following list may be applicable to home-run businesses:

Setting up

Sole trader

As a sole trader you are wholly responsible for your business and its dealings and you are also personally responsible for all debts incurred and your personal possessions, e.g. your home, may have to be sold to cover your debts.

Trade name

You can be a sole trader but you may wish to use a trade name, for example 'Quick and Sure Builders'. You cannot use the word 'Limited' unless your business is incorporated and registered. A list of prohibited names is available from Companies House★ (or Companies Registry★ in Northern Ireland) – that is, names that

Where to obtain your licence

Business	Licence from
Auction saleroom (held in your barn?)	local authority
Betting agency (bookmaker's permit)	local magistrate
Billiard/snooker rooms	local magistrate
Bingo hall (that barn again?)	local authority
Café/restaurant/tea room	Environmental Health Department
Caravan site	local authority
Children's nursery	Social Services Department
Cinema or theatre	local authority
Ear Piercing/Body piercing/ Tattooing/Acupuncture	Environmental Health Department
Employment agency	DfEE
Food manufacturer	Environmental Health Department
Dealer in or hirer of fruit machines	local authority
Hairdresser	local authority
Hire company (of machinery, tools etc.)	Office of Fair Trading
Massage parlour	local authority
Mobile food shop	Environmental Health Department
Nursing agency	Social Services Department
Nursing home	Social Services Department
Pet shop/kennels/cattery etc.	Environmental Health Department
Riding establishment	local authority
Selling alcohol (in your café)	local magistrate
Scrap-metal dealer	local authority
Street trader	local authority (police)
Theatrical agency	DfEE

are not allowed by law such as Royal, Trust, Association and so on. You will probably have to appoint a specialist company or a firm of solicitors to apply for you to use a specific name, which must not be the same as another company in existence. You do not have to submit accounts to Companies House. The law affecting company directors under the Companies Act does not apply to sole traders.

Partnership

For a partnership of two or more people, the same rules apply as for sole traders. A partnership agreement has to be drawn up by a solicitor because you have to apportion profits and losses. You also have to commit to paper your agreement for cheque-signing, partners leaving or joining, financial arrangements and so on. Under the law, all partners are liable for the debts of the business, even if they are 'sleeping' (non-working) partners.

Limited company

A company must have at least two shareholders, one director and a company secretary, who could be a second director. If the company cannot pay its debts the shareholders are liable to pay an amount equal to the nominal value of their shares. Setting up a limited company has to be done through a solicitor because a statutory form of incorporation has to be sworn in. The directors of the company are subject to various legal constraints which make them personally responsible for any illegal activity or negligence by their company, even if it was unknown to them at the time. If a company director gives a personal guarantee for a company's bank loan he or she will be personally liable for the full amount in the event of the company going bust. Unlike the company, he or she will not be covered for limited liability.

The law states that the accounts of a limited company have to be professionally audited each year and the annual accounts have to be submitted to Companies House (Companies Registry in Northern Ireland) to be available for public scrutiny. Directors' meetings must be properly minuted and shareholders must have an annual meeting.

Buying an existing business

The main thing to note if you are buying a business is that, if it has employees, the new owner must maintain their existing conditions of employment and their employee rights (see Chapter 13).

Co-operatives

There are two types of co-operative. Under the Industrial and Provident Societies Acts 1965-78 an Industrial and Provident Co-operative must have at least three members. Under the Companies Act 1985 a limited company co-operative need only have two members. The principles, however, are the same. Every employee who is a member owns one share of the business, everybody has equal voting rights and the profits are shared.

Health and safety

This is probably the major area where you can fall foul of the law because since 1974 various Acts of Parliament have introduced regulations which address the health and safety of employees at work, the health and safety of children and the elderly in specific places such as nurseries and nursing homes (see Chapter 12). In addition, there are many regulations which are designed to protect the consumer from bad hygiene, faulty goods and lack of fire safety. For further information contact the Environmental Health Services of your local council.

Food safety

The whole area of food safety is a minefield. You must be prepared to invest time, patience and money getting it right and complying with all the regulations.

The Food Safety Directorate of the Ministry of Agriculture, Fisheries and Food (MAFF) is responsible for ensuring that food is safe for human consumption right from the farm or garden through to the processing and packaging. For instance, the Directorate controls the quantity and type of pesticides used, and makes regular checks on harmful chemicals, radioactivity or poisonous metals that could contaminate or come into contact with anything produced on a farm, market garden or fish farm. It also enforces regulations on what food additives may be used, and monitors whether the packaging is safe or whether it may leave residues on the food or drink.

The local authorities, in the form of Environmental Health Officers, then take over to ensure that food prepared further along the chain, in commercial or domestic kitchens, is safe and that food sold in shops complies with all necessary legislation. Legislation covers, amongst other things, such areas as the temperature at which food must be stored, the type of utensils to be used, the system for disposing of waste, the cleaning of walls, worktops and equipment, the banning of animals from food preparation areas, and the personal hygiene of those preparing food.

Food Safety (General Food Hygiene) Regulations 1995

These regulations affect anyone who owns, manages or works in a food business. They apply to anything from a sandwich van to a restaurant, from a village hall where food is prepared to a supermarket. These regulations cover every process which deals with the preparation and sale of food including: processing, manufacturing, transportation, distribution, handling, packaging, storage, selling and supplying. They do not apply to food cooked at home for private consumption. Wherever food is sold two basic rules always apply:

CASE HISTORY: Ranjit

Ranjit and his wife make bhajis and samosas and deliver them to shops and garages as snack food. Ranjit had to have his kitchen inspected by the Environmental Health Officer and it had to be refurbished to comply with the regulations. New tiling, a new sink, a new refrigerator and extra ventilation cost Ranjit almost £2,000. He was told that his products would have to be packaged according to the regulations with detailed labelling, listing ingredients, storage instructions and so on. Ranjit bought a machine that heat-sealed polythene packets and he prints out the labels on his computer. Fortunately, after all that investment, the business is doing well and showing a profit. The kitchen facilities have to be regularly inspected and Ranjit has set aside a sum to allow for yearly refurbishment.

- there should always be adequate facilities to prepare and serve food safely;
- food handling procedures should avoid exposing food to risk of any contamination.

For further advice about the regulations, contact the Environmental Health services of your local council.

Food Safety Act 1990

The Food Safety Act empowers Environmental Health Officers to enter food premises uninvited and to inspect the food and the premises, to take samples away for investigation and if necessary to ask a Justice of the Peace to condemn food as unfit for human consumption. They may demand that improvements be made to premises that they consider unhygienic and, if those improvements

---

CASE HISTORY: Patricia

Patricia runs a wedding and celebrations catering business. She plans the menus with the clients, buys in the food and her workers (casual staff) prepare the food on the day at the venue (village hall or social club). Patricia only caters for functions that are taking place at halls where she knows the kitchens have been approved by the Environmental Health Department. However, one afternoon an inspector made a spot check on her operations and was not pleased with what he saw. His report stated that raw and cooked food was being prepared in the same area: one helper had a cut on her finger which was not covered with a waterproof dressing; food that had been prepared for the buffet had not been covered up – it was just in open bowls or on plates on the worktop; one helper was smoking in a room adjacent to the food preparation and the door was open; the refrigerator where the cold meats were stored was not functioning to the required temperature. The Environmental Health Officer advised Patricia that unless she employed people with food hygiene training or sent her existing staff to be trained, he would close her business down. She had no choice but to send her five regular staff for two days' training each and to change her working habits.

---

are not made, or if the state of the premises is bad, they may close a business down very quickly. It can only be reopened when the local authority certifies that it is no longer a threat to public health. (There is a right of appeal and the right to compensation if a business has been wrongfully penalised.)

The Food Safety Act covers the safety of food from its point of origin (farm or garden, say) right through to its point of sale. You break the law if you sell or manufacture food that:

- is unfit for human consumption, for example produce that is rotten, mildewed or contains chemicals or additives that have been ruled unfit for human consumption
- is rendered injurious to health, for example by poor sterilisation of equipment
- is so contaminated that it would be unreasonable to expect it to be eaten, for example food that has become tainted by the flavour or smell of another substance stored close by
- is not of the nature, substance or quality demanded by the purchaser, for example jam which has not set properly or is not covered by a proper lid
- is falsely or misleadingly represented, for example something labelled 'chocolate cake' which contains no chocolate
- is sold after its 'use by' date, in the case of any highly perishable food which has, by law, to be marked with a 'use by' date. (It is not illegal to sell food once its 'best before' datemark has expired – the mark merely alerts you to the possibility that the food may be past its best)
- is sold in contravention of any other type of datemarking, including the falsification of a datemark.

Organic produce

The production and sale of organic foods is controlled by European and UK legislation which applies to every stage, from farming practices to packing and labelling. Organic growers, processors and importers must be registered and regularly inspected. In the UK, the United Kingdom Register of Organic Food Standards (UKROFS)* administers the regulation and carries out inspections with six other certification bodies, including the Scottish Organic Producers Association (SOPA).*

CASE HISTORY: Doreen

Doreen keeps ducks and sells the eggs 'at the garden gate' of her home. She knows that as long as she sells her eggs on a casual basis in this manner she does not have to label or weigh them. She may not put them in other people's boxes, nor may she sell cracked or deformed eggs. Doreen decided to invest in a stock of 100 plain six-egg boxes and had some basic stationery labels printed with her name and address and telephone number, which she sticks on the corner of the box. This has two purposes: she complies with the regulations for commercial egg sales in that she provides her name and address to the customer and, also, customers can ring her to see if she has any eggs available before they make the trip out to her house. She is also required to stamp every box with the date when the eggs were laid.

Organic farmers follow a set of principles which aim to minimise damage to the environment and wildlife. They use crop rotation and natural fertilisers to help soil fertility and often grow a mixture of plant varieties in fields to help control the spread of pests and disease. The result is that organic food is produced without the use of artificial fertilisers or chemical pesticides and it does not contain genetically modified ingredients.

Organic meat has to come from animals that are treated with concern for their welfare. They are given antibiotics and conventional medicines only when there is no alternative.

If you want to grow and market organic produce you should contact the Soil Association,★ which will give you information about what is required to bring your production up to the necessary levels to earn Soil Association approval. After rigorous inspection you may be allowed to display the Soil Association symbol on your products.

Toys

The regulations covering the safety of children's toys are quite extensive. First, certain products are not regarded as toys for the purpose of the regulations, although they may be subject to their own safety regulations. Such items include Christmas decorations, fashion jewellery for children, detailed scale models and jigsaw puzzles with more than 500 pieces (or without a picture) that are intended for adult specialists, folk dolls and other decorative dolls intended for collectors, sports equipment, air guns and air pistols, slings and catapults, certain video toys, toy steam engines and babies' dummies. If there is any chance that they might be mistaken for a toy, they must be clearly marked with the words 'This is not a toy'.

The Toys (Safety) Regulations state that there are several areas of risk that have to be guarded against with toys, including the construction of the toy. You can cover these areas by asking yourself the following questions: Where are the toy's weak points? If it gets broken, will a dangerous component such as a nail or screw be exposed? Are there any sharp edges, protrusions, cords, cables or fastenings that might pose a risk? Could a small toy be swallowed by a very young child? If a toy heats up could it become overheated? Could the child or part of the body become trapped inside the toy? Does the packaging present a risk of suffocation?

The regulations also cover the flammability of toys, the chemical and electrical properties of their components and their labelling. For example, toys which might easily be swallowed must be marked 'Not suitable for children under three years'; and functional toys – scaled-down versions of adult appliances – must bear a warning that the toy should be used only under the direct supervision of an adult. Activity toys must be accompanied by instructions with diagrams for correct assembly, and potentially dangerous toys carry instructions of action to be taken in case of an accident.

The making of stuffed toys is popular among homeworkers. Any toys made for small children (who are likely to put them in their mouths) must be made from colourfast, non-toxic materials, and all stuffings must be of low flammability. The biggest problem relating to stuffed toys is that eyes and noses can be removed. Guidelines issued by WI Country Markets recommend that features on toys for very small children are embroidered, while safety eyes should be used for toys for older children. There are also guidelines on packaging for such toys.

Since January 1990 all toys manufactured in Europe, or imported from outside the EU must carry the 'CE' mark which shows that the toy has been manufactured to the required safety standard. The name, trade mark and address of the manufacturer must appear on the packaging.

If you think that all this is over-cautious, note that lack of compliance with the Toys (Safety) Regulations can mean three months' imprisonment or a fine of up to £2,000. For full details of how to go about making toys that comply with the law, seek advice from your local Trading Standards Office (the address will be in the *Yellow Pages*).

Copyright

Remember also the laws of copyright: if you are selling toys for personal gain, even if it is only at a local craft fair, you may not reproduce character toys (Paddington Bear, Winnie-the-Pooh, Noddy and so on) as the rights to the sale of these characters belong to their creators and their merchandisers. Any knitting or sewing patterns sold for these character toys are for private creation only, not for resale. (See also later in the chapter under 'Protection of intellectual property'.)

Clothing

According to EU guidelines, all garments *should* carry labels which show the following:

- the name of the manufacturer or the trade name
- the size of the garment
- the country of origin
- the fabric and percentages, for example, 25% cotton, 75% polyester
- washing/cleaning instructions
- any special warnings, for example 'wash dark colours separately'.

However, nightwear and babywear *must* comply with the above guidelines. Children's nightdresses, nightshirts, dressing gowns and bathrobes (except bathrobes made from 100 per cent terry towelling) must be made of slow-burning fabrics (to British Standard 5722). If you are making such garments, you must purchase a fabric that has passed the low flammability test and ask your supplier for a copy of the certificate.

Children's pyjamas, bathrobes made from 100 per cent terry towelling, all adults' nightwear and all clothes for babies up to three months old must carry a permanent label stating whether or not the garment has passed the low flammability test. If it has, the label should read 'Low Flammability to BS 5722'. Because low flammability does not mean fireproof, the label may also read 'KEEP AWAY FROM FIRE'. If it has not passed the low flammability test, the garment should have a label saying 'KEEP AWAY FROM FIRE'.

Any nightwear that is treated with flame-retardant chemicals must carry a label with the words 'Do not wash at more than 50°C. Check suitability of washing agent'. Any advertisements of such clothing including purchase by mail order must give information about the flammability performance of each garment featured. The Department of Trade and Industry is also very particular about the size and style of the print used on the labels, so if you are planning to develop a nightwear or baby clothes business, get as much advice as possible from your local Trading Standards Office.

Furniture

The Furniture and Furnishings (Fire) (Safety) Regulations 1988 (as amended) apply to:

- domestic upholstered furniture, including sofabeds and children's furniture
- nursery furniture containing upholstery
- garden furniture containing upholstery
- scatter cushions and seat pads
- pillows
- secondary covers for upholstered furniture (loose and stretch covers)
- cover fabric and filling material supplied for use with furniture and furnishings (including DIY use).

Please note that this is not a definitive list.

If you supply any of the above, as a manufacturer, upholsterer, importer, wholesaler, retailer or auctioneer, you need to understand

189

the full implications of the regulations. The regulations also apply to the hire of furniture and furniture in accommodation – which affects anyone in the renting business.

Pillows, scatter cushions, seat pads, baby nests, secondary covers for upholstered furniture, beds and mattresses should have labels permanently attached which explain about flammability.

Other new furniture must carry two labels – one permanent, the other a swing ticket. The ticket gives basic notice of compliance with fire tests and carries the warning 'Carelessness causes fire'.

As with toys, the furniture and upholstery labels have to comply with certain standards and it is best to seek advice from your Trading Standards Office.

Consumer Protection Act 1987

A consumer can sue a manufacturer, importer or any person who puts his or her name to a product if a defective product causes death, injury or damage to property valued at more than £275.

The producer of the goods (any of the three categories mentioned above) is liable unless he or she can prove the following:

- He or she did not supply the goods (for example they were stolen or forged).
- When the product was manufactured the scientific or technological state of knowledge was such that the defect was not discoverable; the defect took some time to surface and it was only obvious that it would occur at some point with the benefit of hindsight and advanced knowledge (this is known as the development risks defence).
- The defect was attributable to the law. Say, for example, a manufacturer of toys used a special non-toxic paint on his product in order to comply with the EU regulations on such matters, but subsequently that paint reacted with the base material and caused cracks to appear in the product. This caused sharp edges in the toy and it cut a child's face.
- The defect was caused after it left the producer's hands, for example a retailer mishandled or badly stored the product and caused the defect.

- The supplier is not in business but is a private individual. Trading Standards Departments will make an exception in the case of individuals who supply home-made toys to bazaars and fêtes and individuals who sell second-hand goods.
- The defect was caused at a later stage in the manufacturing process of the whole product.

CASE HISTORY: Kelly

Kelly made cosmetics to a very high standard in her own kitchen. She sold rosewaters, orange flower waters, bath essences, bath oils and so on with great success. However, one day she was contacted by the Environmental Health Department and was subsequently fined quite heavily because a customer who was allergic to lanolin had suffered a painful rash on her skin as a result of using Kelly's face cream. The product contained lanolin but Kelly had omitted to put that fact on the label because she did not realise that the regulations demanded it.

Supply of Goods and Services Act 1982

Goods sold must:

- be of satisfactory quality (they must be fit to sell)
- be fit for the purpose for which they are being sold (if an item is sold as an umbrella, then it must perform the functions of an umbrella)
- correspond with the description (if the advertisement says that this product will do certain things and it does not, it is not what was described).

If the goods are not any of the above, then the customer has a right to claim compensation. However, if any defect was brought to the customer's attention before he or she purchased (for example, fire-damaged material in a sale), he or she has no right to expect compensation in relation to that particular defect. Also, if a customer asked if, say, a certain tool would be right for a certain job and was told that it probably would not, he or she has no right to a refund if he or she chose to ignore the sales person.

Services must be provided:

- with reasonable care
- with reasonable skill
- within a reasonable time
- at a reasonable charge.

A trader can be sued for breach of contract if it is proved that he or she failed to exercise reasonable care or reasonable skill. Under the Unfair Contract Terms Act 1977 a trader cannot exclude or limit his or her liability for death or personal injury arising from negligence.

Data Protection Act 1998

This Act requires anyone who keeps personal information on other people to register with the Data Protection Registrar★ and explain the use to which this information will be put. The Act also gives private individuals the right of access to the information held on them in order to check its accuracy.

You may find yourself in the position of being a self-employed teleworker who amends mailing lists or credit information. This would constitute personal data which would have to be registered. The Act also, in some measure, safeguards against this data being misused (see page 138).

Protection of intellectual property

Ideas, inventions and designs should all be protected by registration. The Patents Act 1977 allows any object that has been invented and is capable of commercial application to be patented. It is advisable to do this through a patent agent because the papers necessary for an application for a patent, are, in fact, legal documents. Patents have to be taken out around the world in order to protect an invention from being copied (see pages 147–8). The protection lasts for 20 years and is renewable. It is possible, of course, to market an invention that has not yet been patented while the application is pending. 'Patent pending' is seen on many gadgets and devices.

Designs can be registered, provided the design is not merely an inevitable consequence of the function of the object and makes some appeal to the eye (for example, the design of a car). At least 50 of the items must be manufactured or produced before a design can be registered. Purely functional designs that are not attractive enough to merit registration may have some protection as unregistered designs.

Trade marks – logos, designs or names adopted by companies to make their products or service memorable – can be registered at the Patent Office.* No one else can use them once they are registered.

Copyright of written material, films, music, works of art, software and industrial designs and drawings is not something that is registered. It is automatic if you create something original, and generally last for 70 years following the author of the work's death. It is recommended that you put the copyright sign, the date and your name on each piece of work that you create. Copyright holders can exploit the right by selling copies of the work or by licensing someone else to do so in return for a fee, usually called a royalty. You can sue another individual or an organisation if you feel that they have 'copied' your original piece of work or reproduced it without your permission.

Ownership of intellectual property

The owner of a new work is usually the person who wrote it. Self-employed people usually own the copyright but if an employee creates the work, ownership will turn on whether the work was created in the course of employment.

Conclusion

There are too many rules and regulations to cover them all in one chapter of this book; the above are just those that might be of most interest to someone setting up a small business or working for themselves. Tax and VAT matters, mail order and employment legislation are dealt with elsewhere in this book, and Chapter 12 deals exclusively with legislation pertaining to converting your home or land into a business.

Chapter 11

Your business relationships

Customers, clients, agents, suppliers, employees – all must be kept happy and it is sometimes the 'people' side of business that is the most difficult to handle. However, if you can cultivate good business relationships they can be worth their weight in gold – to be able to have confidence in a colleague, to have a rapport based on mutual respect and trust, can be like a good marriage. In view of how much of your daily time you have to devote to work, the relationships arising from it are very important.

Relationships with your customers

This can be the most unpredictable area of your business relationships. After all, your dealings with agents, employees, suppliers and so on are controlled to a certain extent by contracts which state how you will all perform. You cannot do that with customers – or can you?

You can, in fact, draw up some sort of contract which customers and clients have to respect. It is your terms of trading – in other words, what you contract to supply and how they must pay for it. It can be a note of agreement between yourself and a client, a notice pinned up in your workshop or a statement of terms printed on your invoice. You can clarify the relationship between you and your customer in several ways.

Confirmation of an oral contract

Suppose you go to meet a potential client and he offers you a project. You discuss the requirements of the job, the payment and the timescale over a drink in a pub. There are no witnesses. He may be

---

CASE HISTORY: Tanya

Tanya is a registered childminder who looks after several children at different times during the week. She presents all her parents with a form which they sign before she takes charge of their children. It gives permission for the children in her care to be taken out shopping, to be taken in the car (suitably fastened in), to be allowed to watch children's television for an hour or so, to be reprimanded if naughty and so on. She also asks the parents to give her a complete list of dietary requirements for the children and insists that parents telephone if they will be delayed in picking up their child. Also, for safety reasons, she requires a named person to be available to pick up the child if the child becomes ill when parents are out at work. These 'regulations' may seem rather pedantic but Tanya enjoys a very good relationship with all her customers because everyone knows exactly what the rules are and they are happy with them.

---

a very nice man and you may feel instinctively that you can trust him, but there could have been a misunderstanding over some of the finer points of the project you are about to embark upon. So when you get home you should immediately commit to paper your understanding of the terms and conditions of the job on offer and send it to him for his confirmation. That way, everyone is happy with what was discussed. You have a written contract.

Explanation of payment terms

If you are selling products directly to the public, whether door-to-door, by mail order, from a stall, or in your own shop, you must make it very clear to the customers what forms of payment are acceptable. Notices like 'Cash sales only' or 'Sorry, we cannot accept credit cards' or 'Cheques only accepted for amounts over £10' must be prominently displayed or printed on your literature.

If you are working from home and just starting out, you cannot afford to lose control of your cash flow. That means that you must have money coming in – real money, not promised money – before you can afford to invest more money in building up your stock.

Right at the beginning you have to decide what your payment terms are going to be. If you are selling from a stall in a market then your payment is instantaneous – or at least it should be. If a cheque is incorrectly filled in or it bounces, you are in trouble. Therefore, insist on the cheque being backed by a guarantee card (some still cover £50 but many now cover £100), or at the very least ask for the customer's name, address and telephone number to be written on the back of the cheque, and write these down in a book before you present the cheque to your own bank in case it bounces. That way you will know where to get hold of the customer to demand another payment or your goods back.

CASE HISTORY: Harry

Harry makes beautiful nursery furniture which is custom-made for each child, with the appropriate name carved into it. He therefore insists on a deposit on an article before he starts work, then an approval visit by the customer before the child's name is put on the item of furniture, with a further payment at that point. For his part, Harry promises to complete the work within a specified time and guarantees the item of furniture for two years.

If you are starting a new venture you might find it wise to trade on a 'cash only' basis. Banks now charge business accounts a fee for each cheque processed and many small shopkeepers, for example, now refuse to take payment by cheque for sums less than £10.

Selling door-to-door is the same, unless you are selling such a large range of stock that you cannot carry it all with you and products have to be ordered. In this case you want an order form signed by the purchaser, which is, in effect, a binding contract with the customer before you order the goods. Note that customers are entitled to a 'cooling-off' period if you sell to them in their own home. During this period they are allowed, by law, to change their minds (see Chapter 9).

When starting a mail-order business, it is sensible to ask for payment up front if possible. You cannot afford to 'sell from a distance' without some guarantee of payment. In return, you have to offer a trial period with full cash-back rights if the product is not suitable. Most small mail-order concerns operate in this way – you have to

---

CASE HISTORY: Alison

Alison makes designer wedding dresses, none of which are exactly alike. She therefore charges her clients a separate fee for the drawing up of the design. When they have approved the design and selected the material, she asks for a one-third deposit of the total cost of the dress. This pays for all the materials and trimmings. She then insists on several fittings and the final two-thirds payment before the trimmings are put on. Sadly, some of her clients have called off their weddings because their relationships have broken up, but Alison takes the view that they will undoubtedly find another partner and can therefore keep the wedding dress in the wardrobe for the next occasion!

---

be a very large going concern before you can afford to part with goods and wait for payments to come in in stages. It would be prudent to acquaint yourself fully with the Advertising Standards Authority (ASA)★ code applying to selling by mail order. This is available on request from the ASA.

Credit cards

These are an increasing problem nowadays for small traders. Credit cards are being used more and more to pay for purchases, to the extent that some people rarely carry cheque books or cash. Being able to accept the major credit cards can boost your sales enormously and it is, of course, guaranteed and 'instant' payment. So at what point in your business activities do you start accepting credit cards?

Unfortunately, it may not be up to you. Because of the prevalence of fraud in recent years the credit card companies have become more particular about accreditation – particularly if you want telephone or postal facilities, because these are, apparently, the most vulnerable areas of fraud. This is a pity, because most small mail-order businesses would dearly love to have a credit-card facility. Another problem is that there is a certain amount of prejudice by the credit card operators against home-run businesses (they feel that they lack credibility and stability) and they also prefer to do business with traders who have been operating for at least a year and can provide a copy of one year's accounts as proof of creditworthiness.

A credit card facility, of course, costs you money, which you have to build into your prices. As well as an initial registration fee, which can vary between credit card companies but is around £300 on average, a small trader can pay up to five per cent on every transaction. Some credit card companies offer the first six months of trading free, as an incentive. You can charge extra for credit card transactions over cash or cheques, so there may be scope for passing on those costs to customers who value the facility. However, if you cannot build this into your price because the competition is too fierce, this five per cent is quite a large chunk out of your profits.

Debit cards

Debit cards, such as Visa Delta or Switch, were introduced to replace cheques, rather than credit cards. They are plastic cards which the purchaser presents to the trader who debits the purchaser's bank account for the necessary amount via a computer terminal. It can take up to two days for the amount to be debited from the purchaser's account, whereas a cheque can take up to five working days. The advantages to the trader are no more bouncing cheques or bad debts. It is as good as cash to the trader.

Until recently, a debit card facility was not really an option for small businesses because of the cost of purchasing or renting the computer equipment to effect the transaction. But small hand-held terminals are now available and it is no longer uncommon to see even street market vendors offering debit facilities.

Offering such a facility is, up to a certain point, cheaper than operating a credit card facility. Credit card companies charge a percentage on every purchase. Debit card transactions are done on a flat fee basis. Therefore, if you provide high-cost goods or services or operate a business where customers buy in bulk from you on one purchase, a debit card transaction will cost you less than a credit card transaction. It is impossible to quote even an average fee for the service as debit card facilities are all operated through 'providers', in other words, most of the high-street banks, which all charge different rates and offer different deals. At the time of writing, some of the providers are restricting debit card facilities to companies who achieve a certain level of turnover but the indications are that they are becoming more flexible. It is worth discussing it with your bank manager to see whether it is a viable option for your business.

Credit terms

If you are prepared to offer credit terms (rather risky for a fledgling business, but you may have no option), you must take several steps first.

If the customer is another business, you must check his or her creditworthiness. Ask for references from other suppliers, wholesalers or even the customer's bank, and check them thoroughly. Ask the other suppliers if they give the customer in question credit terms and, if so, for how long, and whether they have ever had any trouble with payments.

If the potential customer is a very large enterprise, it is worth paying one of the credit-rating agencies to check on the company for you. Alternatively, you can purchase a copy of its accounts from Companies House* for £7.50. This will show the health of its finances at the date of the most recent balance sheet. In order to check the current situation, you need to try to speak to some of the company's suppliers and customers to find out if the bills are being paid. You probably cannot afford to let smaller business customers have more than the standard 28 or 30 days' credit before payment is due.

Incentives

The most significant incentive you can offer any customer is a discount for a cash payment or prompt payment. It may be worth it to you to offer, say, five per cent off the normal price of a product just to get an instant payment of real cash, or for a business customer to settle ahead of the usual 30 days' credit period.

Customers' rights

Apart from the statutory obligations that you will provide customers, in good faith, with goods that have no defects and are fit for the purpose for which they are described and, in the case of service, that you will exercise reasonable care and skill and will do the job in a reasonable time, the customer has a right to expect several other things.

Courtesy

Everyone has the right to expect that they will be treated with courtesy when they are doing business with you. There may be a few eccentric artists or crafts people who can get away with being surly and taciturn and still sell their work, but it would be rash to count on being able to do that yourself. 'The customer is king' goes the saying, and it is right; without customers, you don't do any business. Saying, 'Can I help you?' when they are browsing round your workshop goes a long way. Similarly, a 'thank you' when they have completed their purchase costs you nothing and means a lot.

Attention

Customers have the right, first of all, to be able to get your attention. How many times have you stood at a shop counter or sat in a café and fumed while two assistants carry on a personal conversation and ignore you? Secondly, customers have the right to expect your attention to detail. If they want to give you instructions as to how a service should be carried out, they will expect you to pay attention – even write it down – so that you can get the job right. If you are making a product, customers have the right to expect that you have given it your full attention and not skimped or made mistakes. If they ask for your professional opinion on whether a certain product will do the job they have in mind, they have a right to expect that you have given some attention to learning about the products you are selling and can advise with expertise.

Friendliness

Customers are encouraged by smiles. If customers at a craft fair have a choice between two stalls selling cushions, the one with the stallholder who smiles and chats will always win out over the gloomy one. However, friendly chitchat can be overdone – if there are customers queuing up some may become impatient and go elsewhere.

Efficiency

Customers have the right to expect, particularly when ordering through the post or over the telephone, that the order will be despatched quickly and efficiently. Similarly, all queries and accounts should be dealt with efficiently. You may be the most charming salesman or woman in the world but if your paperwork is a mess and you have no filing system, you will lose customers because they have been frustrated by your lack of organisation.

Action

If a customer has a justifiable complaint he or she has a right to expect some action. If you are working from home on your own, you are the boss and the buck stops with you. Junior personnel might be able to get away with saying 'I'll have to ask the manager', but you can't. You have to learn to make quick decisions and act upon them.

Dealing with complaints

You will get complaints – some reasonable, some unreasonable. Some you can deal with and resolve amicably, others you cannot. The main thing is that you must, if you are going to work for yourself, develop a thick skin. You cannot afford to treat each complaint as a personal insult and lose your temper. You must be able to admit that you, or one of your staff, has made a mistake and be able to apologise and take action.

Some customers are troublemakers – they are never happier than when they are complaining. Keep a cool head and refuse to get angry, even if the person gets abusive. This frequently happens on the telephone. If you have an angry customer in person in your workshop, try to take him or her aside, somewhere quiet, away from other customers, to resolve the matter.

If the customer has returned the product which has broken or is defective, you must establish whether he or she wants a replacement or a refund. Bear in mind that, in most cases, the customer is entitled to a full refund and does not have to accept a replacement product unless he or she specifically wishes to do so. If the customer has bought the wrong product because one of your staff advised him or her badly, you have no choice but to exchange or refund.

If the customer wishes to return a product for a less valid reason, for example she thought the jumper would match a skirt but it did not, you must explain, in a friendly manner, that she should have brought the skirt with her when buying the jumper and that as the jumper is of perfectly good quality you are under no obligation to change it or refund money. If she is a very good and regular customer, it is up to you whether you allow her, just this once, to change the item. In practice, most retailers do allow exchanges and refunds but, if you are a very small retailer you can reserve the right to adopt a firm policy.

If you provide a service and you have plainly fallen down in the quality of that service, the customer has the right to an amended bill or to have the work done again free. If you have caused irreparable damage by your poor service, the customer has the right to sue you for full compensation. You could settle out of court, but the legal procedures for this are still expensive and time-consuming.

From the very beginning of your new enterprise it is prudent to print, perhaps on your receipts or invoices, the terms and conditions under which you will accept responsibility for the return of goods or non-payment of services. Remember that these terms and conditions must comply with the law. The customer must produce proof of purchase but you cannot specify the production of a till receipt before you will refund the money, nor can you insist on replacement goods rather than a refund. Draw your customer's attention to the terms and conditions when making the sale or agreeing to provide a service. Don't make a rod for your own back with such promises as: 'If you can get this product cheaper anywhere else we will refund the difference' – only the major department stores can afford to do that. Similarly, never make claims for your service that you may not be able to keep because of changing circumstances, such as 'guaranteed 24-hour turnaround on all jobs'. This will give the customer the right to refuse payment if you take a bit longer.

Listen to customers

When a customer does complain, try to learn from it. Complaints can be a positive aid to your business. Try to view it as a method of quality control for your business. If, for example, you are running a mail-order business selling products that you buy in rather than make yourself, you should review your product range if one particular item causes a certain number of complaints.

If your attitude or the attitude of your staff causes complaints, you must do something about it. If your service is sloppy and meets with dissatisfaction, you need to rethink what you are doing. Perhaps you should concentrate on providing those services you can do really well? Perhaps you are trying to do too much yourself and need some assistance? Would you benefit from some refresher training? Do your staff need some customer relation training?

What customers say is a continuing source of market research. Their ideas, preferences, tastes and irritations will point the way for you to improve your product range or service. But you must listen to them. It is too easy to get caught up in the day-to-day business of earning money and to dismiss comments made by customers during the course of work.

Occasionally it is worth conducting a small survey among your customers to find out if they are satisfied with your efforts. Use the mailing list you have compiled of all your customers. (Compiling mailing lists is covered in more detail in Chapter 8.) Even if you sell from a stall you can invite cash customers to write down their name and address in a book if they would like further information about your products. By building up a mailing list you can then, at some point, include a short questionnaire (with a stamped addressed envelope) and invite comments about what products customers are particularly interested in, what times of year they purchase, how much they are prepared to spend and so on.

Bad debts

This is the unpleasant side of customer relations – when the agreement has broken down and the customer has failed to pay. This is not a problem, of course, for strictly cash-on-the-nail businesses, but many sole traders have to rely on the invoice system and it can be heartbreaking, not to mention hazardous, for a very small business when a customer does not co-operate.

If you have tried without success to get the customer to pay by making phone calls and writing letters, the next step is to appoint a solicitor to write a letter threatening legal action. If this fails, you have to decide whether to write off the bad debt or whether it is worth pursuing it through the courts.

In April 1999 the civil justice system is to be completely reformed. There will be three levels of court action based, principally, on the value of the case, but they are supposed to be flexible.

The first level will be a small claims procedure for cases worth up to £5,000 with a £1,000 limit for personal injury and housing disrepair cases. Eviction and harassment cases will be excluded. The court proceeding will be informal, lawyers will not be necessary and legal representation costs will not be recoverable.

The second level will be for cases worth up to £15,000 and this level is, supposedly, going to operate a 'fast track' system to cut down on waiting time. The procedure in the court will be slightly more complex, with some reference to the rules of giving evidence and, it is thought, that legal representation will be advisable.

The third level will be for cases which, by their complex nature or the sums of money involved, require 'hands-on judicial case management' (in other words, some personal attention). A basic set of rules will cover both the county courts and the High Court but, at the time of writing, these had not been made available. Neither have the intended fees and charges for those bringing actions for debt recovery been published.

How can customers be made to pay up?

If a court decides in your favour, you can choose from the following methods of recovering your money but you will have to pay more fees for these services.

Garnishee order   The court orders a debtor of your debtor to pay his or her money directly to you rather than to your debtor.

A warrant of execution   Sending the bailiffs in to take away any of your client's goods which he or she fully owns, and the sale of which will cover the debt to you.

Attachment of earnings   This can be of use only where the debtor is a salaried employee because the order instructs the debtor's employer to deduct regular sums from his or her wages and pay them directly to you.

Charging order   The court makes an order which, in effect, means that if your debtor sells his or her house or land, what is owed to you has to be deducted from the proceeds of the sale.

If you are in doubt about any of the above procedures contact your local Citizens Advice Bureau for advice. Obviously, if your bad debt is less than £100 there is very little point in spending as much again in pursuing it through the county court. You just have to chalk it up to experience and never do business again with doubtful payers.

Weed out the bad customers

Some customers are just not worth tolerating. For example, one artist regularly sold small paintings to a local woman but her cheques periodically bounced. The customer always rectified the matter but every time one of the cheques bounced, the artist's bank charged her £5. She has since changed her bank to one that does not charge her for other people's bouncing cheques and she has also got tough with the regular customer by saying that she can sell to her only on a cash basis.

If you have a customer who always disputes your invoice, beware – this may be a delaying tactic. Take it as a warning sign that the customer's cash flow is unsteady. It may be prudent to drop him or her.

You should invoice immediately after the service is provided or delivery has been made and you should send a statement as soon as the credit time has elapsed, for example, after 30 days. Find out what the payment timings are. For example, some companies pay by computer and the computer prints all the cheques on the 15th of every month. Therefore, if your invoice has not arrived and/or the data has not been fed into the computer by a certain date, you will not get paid that month, but will have to wait for the next data input.

Always check with your potential customers what their expectation of credit is. You would be amazed at the number of companies that say, 'We never pay on receipt of invoice, only on receipt of statement, it's a company policy.' In other words, they expect 60 days' credit. Other, usually large, companies state flatly that all their suppliers give them 90 days' credit. This is fine if your cash flow can stand it, but you must decide whether doing business with such customers will put too much of a strain on your resources.

Factoring

If your business has expanded successfully and you do not have time to chase up bad payers or even to keep an eye on your credit control situation every month, factoring could be the solution. It is cheaper than paying off an overdraft or hiring someone full-time to chase up invoices.

Factoring means that a specialist company buys all your invoices from you the day that they are sent out, and initially pays you 80 per cent of their total value. You get the bulk of the cash while the factoring company has the headache of chasing up the invoices. When payment is made you get the other 20 per cent, less the interest charged on the 80 per cent paid in advance to you (usually between 3 to 4 per cent above base rate) and an administration charge of around 2 per cent of the total value of the invoices.

Factoring is not an option for everyone because factoring companies are usually only interested in businesses with a turnover of more than £50,000. But that is not so far out of reach for some of the readers of this book – it is not unknown for consultants or specialist teleworkers to make that kind of turnover in a year. Banks can usually provide a list of factoring companies.

When you take on a factoring company you decide just what level of service you want from them. They can chase up all your invoices and they can also manage your sales accounts and run credit checks on potential customers. Bad debts seem to disappear when factoring companies handle accounts. Bad customers tend to respond better to a letter from a factoring company than from a small business.

Relationships with your suppliers

In this instance you are the customer and therefore you need to be reassured about several things.

The supplier's financial health and reputation

If you do not already have a supplier lined up, you can find one from directories of suppliers in a reference library, for example *Kompass Directories*. It is then a question of asking around among other business people or trade associations to see whether that supplier is reputable. A good supplier should be willing to give you the names of regular customers so that you can have a reassuring chat with them. You can, of course, pay for a credit check to be run on a supplier (the same procedure is discussed earlier in this chapter), but this would really only be necessary if supplies from that quarter were so crucial that you could not operate without them.

If it is possible, or relevant to your business, you could check up on the premises of all the major suppliers you are likely to use – you can tell a lot by the way business is conducted there. Are they neat and tidy? Is the order-processing system efficient? Are the staff helpful and well trained? Do they give you unbiased advice? Obviously, if you are buying small quantities of materials from suppliers scattered all over the country, this will not be a viable option.

The supplier's reliability

It can be worth writing to suppliers to explain what your requirements might be, then see what sort of written response you get. If a supplier sends back an impressive reply – that is to say helpful, enclosing price lists and details of services – you should feel confident enough to proceed. If, however, the response is indifferent, the chances are the service will be too. Check with other customers as to whether they have ever had any problems with the supplier's reliability.

The quality of the goods

If you are buying raw materials such as textiles, stuffing or wadding you need to know exactly the composition of the material, its colour fastness, flammability and so on in order that you can buy what is best for your product. You must be assured that similar quality goods will always be available – you do not want to find yourself suddenly without a source at a crucial moment.

The promptness and flexibility of delivery times

If you will need your materials to be delivered it is important that you know how flexible or inflexible the supplier's schedules are. For example, perhaps he or she delivers to your area only on Thursdays and this is not ideal as you require delivery early in the week and possibly more than once a week. Does he or she always deliver on time? Only experience of the delivery service will tell you that. There is nothing more frustrating than having to stay in all day because a delivery time cannot be given and it means that you cannot make any sales appointments for that day. Delivery charges have to be taken into account, too. Perhaps a supplier offers free delivery for orders over a certain size? Can you buy and store such a quantity of goods to make this saving?

Credit terms and discounts

What credit terms will the supplier give you if you supply references? Is there any discount offered for cash and carry, cash on delivery or early payment of invoices? Do the prices include delivery or is that an extra charge? If you are buying large items what warranty is on offer? Does the supplier ever run special offers that might be of value, say two for the price of one on certain lines or discounts for bulk buying?

Location and communication

If you are considering using a supplier who you will need to visit at least twice a week, location is important, and that in itself may eliminate the competition unless suppliers further afield have reliable and efficient communications and are willing to deliver small quantities frequently. Wherever the supplier is (and you may need a specialist supplier who is at the other end of the country and only contactable by phone/post/fax/email), he or she must have good communications and respond promptly. You want to be able to leave messages, send a fax, speak to an efficient member of staff on the telephone and feel confident that your supplier is dealing with your request. You do not want to do business with someone you can never get hold of, or who keeps goods in an anonymous lock-up warehouse which you can view only by appointment, or who does not appear to have any staff, paperwork or detailed information on his or her goods.

Competition

If you are lucky enough to have several suppliers nearby you can afford to shop around and compare prices. It may be that you end up going to one warehouse for cut flowers, say, another for dried flowers and another for florists' accessories.

Any special terms

These can be important when you are starting up. You may not be able to get any credit terms until you are more established and can order in larger quantities. The supplier may have a minimum order rule; below that amount you have to pay cash up front. It is not worth compromising your cash flow by overstocking just to get credit, unless you are absolutely sure that you can shift all your products. With certain 'short-life' goods which have to be bought little and often – such as fresh flowers or fruit and vegetables – you may be able to open an account with the wholesaler which is settled at the end of every month.

Your relationship with your suppliers is more or less the same as your customers' relationship with you. It has to be based on trust, unless proven otherwise, and each of you has an obligation to the other which basically hinges upon open communication, courtesy and an understanding of the terms and conditions under which you are trading with each other.

Your relationship with your bank

'What relationship?' is often the response. Exactly. Do you want to go through your working life having a relationship with your bank that is merely one of debtor and creditor? There is so much more you could develop in the way of a relationship but it needs the combined effort of you and your bank.

First, it is a question of communication again. Banks have been guilty in the past, and some of them still are, of not communicating with their customers. Charges were made or raised without the customers being informed; conditions of loans and overdrafts were changed without prior notice or consultation. A code of practice was introduced in 1992, and updated in July 1997, to improve the service offered by banks and building societies.

However, it is a two-way process. Small businesses and business borrowers must keep the banks informed of their financial progress. There is no point in hiding a financial problem from your bank manager – he or she may be able to help if you discuss it. Some banks have made the provision of information a condition of business.

You can start off a good relationship with a bank or building society by choosing the right place to put your account and get your loan. If your business has relatively few monthly transactions, for example, you are a writer and receive cheques at infrequent intervals, some banks and building societies may offer free banking for longer than one year.

Finding the right account, which does not impose astronomical charges upon you, will get your relationship with your bank off to a good start. Business accounts have much higher charges than personal accounts – if you do not have lots of cash and cheque transactions you may be able to get away with having a personal account for your business.

Try to choose a bank or building society where there is someone available to offer advice. A branch in a large town may have a Small Business Adviser who can help. If you are involved in one of the government schemes or receiving grant aid from another body, you may find that your bank has a member of staff who deals specifically with that sort of account customer. Invite your bank or building society contact to come and view your home and your work, and perhaps to have lunch. But beware! It has been known for a customer to pay for the lunch and then receive a bill for the bank manager's time and a consultancy fee too!

There is a lot of bad feeling about the high-street banks, which has not been eased by the continuing policy of closing small branches and de-personalising large branches by replacing people with cash machines. Business customers seem to get a rough deal with many banks. Few banks offer business accounts and there is far less competition for them than for personal accounts where customers can shop around for the best deal. One small shopkeeper has complained that he has three accounts at his local bank and the manager still does not know his name. It is worth trying to build up a face-to-face relationship with your lending institution.

Make sure that when you take out an overdraft facility or a loan you keep copies of all correspondence from your bank that indicate changes in interest rates and charges. Check your bank statements carefully; if you think you have been overcharged challenge the bank. If you have a complaint, write to the branch or area manager of the bank or building society. If this proves unsatisfactory, take your complaint further by writing to the head office, then to the Banking or Building Societies Ombudsman,★ as appropriate.

Chapter 12

Using your home and land as a money earner

In Chapter 2 we discussed whether it would be your skill, time, effort, ingenuity, specialist knowledge, qualifications or personality that would be your main asset in making money from home – or a combination of those factors. Having read this far in the book, it should come as no surprise to you to learn that you cannot substitute a piece of property or land for any of the above. In fact, if you are going to turn your home or land into a money-earning enterprise you will need all of these in spadefuls.

What could you do to create a feasible business? Let's start with your house; there are various scenarios you could think about.

Your house

For example, your house may be very large – too large for you and your spouse now that the children have left home – but you do not want to move. What are your options?

- Run a business yourself from part of the house
- Turn the whole of the house into a full-time business
- Run a full-time tourist venture which opens up the house to the public
- Run an occasional tourist venture which opens up the house to the public
- Rent part of the house to someone else for their business purposes
- Capitalise on some special occasion or certain times of the year and turn the house over to other people.

Let's examine each of these options in more depth:

Run a business yourself from part of the house

A recent trend amongst cost-conscious businesspeople in America has been to relocate their small businesses from their expensive city-based offices into their own homes – provided their homes are large enough and they have a small number of staff who are amenable to the suggestion. This has been particularly noticeable amongst male business owners in their mid-fifties. After a lifetime of commuting and working long hours, many of these businessmen choose to relocate their businesses into part of their home in order to enjoy their remaining working life and maximise their leisure and family time. It will not be long before this preference develops in the UK, particularly amongst small service companies that have no particular need to be located in an expensive city centre.

Of course, finding yourself rattling around in a big house after the children have left can neatly coincide with your decision to develop a new career, start a small business, or retrain after redundancy or early retirement. If you are in the fortunate position of having paid off the mortgage it makes sense to devote part of the house to your new business – be it office space or a treatment room where your clients visit.

Turn the whole of the house into a full-time business

You may, for example, choose to turn your large house into a residential home for the elderly or handicapped adults or into a small private school. These options would be attempted only by people with the necessary qualifications – although, in theory, it could be possible to appoint a qualified manager to run the enterprise. However, it is more likely that someone would buy a property that was already converted for such a use or buy a large property with a view to converting it.

Taking in lodgers is a full-time venture, even though you may not be cooking for them, as with a bed-and-breakfast business.

In certain areas of the country bedsitting rooms are in huge demand – university towns for example, near major teaching hospitals and in towns with English language colleges for foreign students.

Your local council will advise you on the current standards required for rented accommodation, if you are interested in taking in lodgers.

You will need to approach your insurer before you embark on installing kitchenettes or extra bathrooms for the bedsits. Such conversions will affect the premiums on your buildings insurance.

If you decide to take in only one or two lodgers you could take advantage of the Rent-a-Room Scheme. Under this, you can earn up to £4,250 a year tax-free in rent on furnished accommodation, provided it is in your main residence. This exemption does not apply to rooms used as offices – only to living accommodation. Further details can be obtained from the Inland Revenue* (a leaflet, *Letting your home (including the Rent-a-Room scheme)* (IR87) is available from your local tax office).

CASE HISTORY: Roshni and Amrit

Roshni and Amrit have a very large house in a university town in the north-east of England. When their children left home they decided to convert all the rooms above the ground floor into student bedsits. They obtained advice from the local authority building inspector, the Environmental Health Officer and the Fire Safety Officer before they did the conversions. Each room (there were six former bedrooms) was equipped with a sofa-bed, dining table and chairs, wardrobe, and a mini-kitchen in an alcove. The bathroom and lavatory on each floor was renovated. They also converted two large landing cupboards into shower rooms. Each bedsit is supplied with a fire extinguisher and a fire blanket. Further adjustments had to be made to conform with fire safety regulations. However, despite investing over £80,000 in the conversion, Roshni and Amrit recouped that money in three years and now make considerable profit each year.

Run a full-time tourist venture which opens up the house to the public

The most common approach is running a bed and breakfast or a small hotel from your home. As this involves having people in your home all the time it is probably the hardest transition to make. One minute the house is yours, your pride and joy, so is the lovely garden that you have worked so hard on – the next minute there are strangers disrupting your peace, criticising your wallpaper and sunbathing in your garden when you fancied a few quiet minutes there yourself. Many people prefer to purchase somewhere new to start up their business. But few people realise just how demanding this sort of business can be. The English Tourist Board★ produces a free pack, *First steps in tourism*. This includes the following checklist for people contemplating setting out on this course. To find out if you have the necessary personality and stamina, ask yourself the following questions:

- Are you in good health?
- Can you work long hours – often from 7.a.m. till midnight?
- Do you mind sharing your home with strangers?
- Do you have the full backing of your family?
- Are you adaptable – and can you make decisions on the hop?
- Is your lifestyle dependent on a regular income?
- Have you any relevant experience in dealing with customers?
- Have you good social skills – happy to chat anytime?
- Are you adept at book-keeping and accounts?
- Can you seek and accept advice?
- Are you willing to take a risk?
- Can you plan ahead?

Be honest with yourself. If you can't say 'yes' to the majority of these questions, then perhaps you should think again about starting up a small tourist concern.

According to the English Tourist Board, many people in the past have viewed a small-scale tourist business such as a guesthouse, B & B, or small hotel as an early retirement option, but now more and more people in their thirties and forties consider it a positive mid-life career change. However, the reality is different. The failure rate is very high, with one in four people selling up within three years.

If you have particularly stunning gardens or your property is extensive enough to open a small museum or some other tourist attraction on it, then you might find that you could cope with the public intrusion. Many people with extensive gardens open them to the public for some part of the year. For some of these people, the charge to the public to enjoy the gardens helps to pay for extra help in the garden during autumn and winter. Charging admission to your garden is unlikely to generate a great deal of profit but it may provide a forum for your other activities such as selling plants, crafts or rearing animals. You usually find that gardens and houses open to the public are linked with several other ventures as well.

Another form of full-time tourist venture, which does not involve having people in your home all the time but does require you to comply with regulations, is to turn the front of your house into something like a tea or coffee shop. If you can reconcile yourself to losing the ground floor of your accommodation to this enterprise and you can get planning permission and cope with having to refit your kitchen to accord with health and food safety regulations, then a tea shop may be a possible option. The hours are much shorter than, say, running a full-scale restaurant, which means that you have to open in the evening. The average opening hours for a tea shop are from 10a.m. until 4p.m., which is much more civilised than running a B & B, where you are on call all the time.

CASE HISTORY: Naomi and Richard

Naomi and Richard own a beautiful fifteenth-century house which was once a convent and has extensive gardens and orchards. They realised that in order to pay for the upkeep of the house and gardens they would have to make the property and land pay for itself, as near as possible. Naomi's interest has always been herbs and therefore they decided to create a large medieval-style herb garden and capitalise on the fact that the nuns in the convent used to tend the sick. They invested some money in buying in some herbal products and set up a shop selling those along with plants from the herb garden. They then turned the old refectory into a modest tea room, after consultation with the Environmental Health Department. Further work in the gardens involved re-planting the apple orchard and getting a local manufacturer to press apple juice and cider from the resultant apples. After five years, the business began to show a small profit but the main thing was that it paid for the continued upkeep and occupation of a historic house and gardens.

Running an occasional tourist venture which opens up the house and/or land to the public

Examples of this would be properties which, say, have a large amount of land and can host occasional events (for which they charge rent) such as rock concerts, horticultural shows, horse shows, garden festivals, product launches and so on. Maybe you have a ballroom or magnificent library or entrance hall in your house, which you could rent out for dances and wedding receptions. Or you may have a warm, dry barn, with power supply, etc., which can be rented out for theatre performances, barn dances or flower shows.

If you have a heated indoor swimming-pool you could investigate with the local education authority, social services or health authority whether they would be interested in renting time in your pool for school swimming, handicapped children and hydrotherapy sessions. You would need to seek advice from the Environmental Health Department to ensure that your pool and its surrounds comply with regulations regarding safety and equipment.

Rent part of your house to someone else for their business purposes

This effectively means that you would have to cease to use that part of the house, but, depending on the business that moves in, it may not intrude too much on the rest of the house and your garden. This is obviously made easier if you have a self-contained area of the house, such as a granny annexe. Remember, however, that you may also have to be able to accommodate extra parking of cars; always try to ensure that you are able to get in and out of your own property at all times. You do not want the inconvenience of having to ask someone else's client to move his or her car every time you want to go out. For example, if you decide to set up or rent out space to a children's day nursery, creche or playgroup in your house, be aware that the amount of parking required by parents and carers depositing and collecting children at certain times during the day can be extensive.

Other enterprises that often rent rooms in private houses include medical practitioners, alternative therapists, hairdressers and dog-grooming parlours but less parking space is required for these businesses.

Any of the businesses mentioned above may require your premises to be modified. If you rent space to a hairdresser, a couple of washbasins and an extra power supply would be needed. A children's care facility would need all kinds of equipment. Obviously any incoming business would provide and pay for any modifications, but as the owner of the property you should be very careful that the modifications would not permanently affect your property. For example, if you decided to terminate the arrangement and sell the house as a private residence, you would want the outgoing business tenant to remove all fixtures and fittings and leave the property in a good state of repair. Therefore you should make sure that it is written into the commercial letting agreement that the tenant must install and remove fixtures to your satisfaction at the commencement and termination of the letting period, if required.

All of the enterprises mentioned above would be regularly inspected by the relevant local authority department which also in some cases, licenses them to operate. This may involve the rest of the house if, say, the Fire Safety Officer wanted to satisfy himself that the power supply in the business premises did not compromise the rest of the property and vice versa.

It would be prudent to ask advice before renting out your premises to anyone. Don't forget that you would have to consult with your insurer, who might take a dim view if it discovered, for example, that you were living over a cabinet-making business which stored lots of flammable materials and you did not inform them of this new hazard.

Capitalise on some special occasion or certain times of the year and turn your house over to other people

As the 1999 solar eclipse approaches this option becomes increasingly pertinent. At the time of writing thousands of home-owners in Cornwall and on the Island of Alderney are preparing to rent their homes and land to all the eclipse-watchers who are going to converge on South-West of England. Unfortunately solar eclipses from which you can profit are few and far between, but other opportunities exist particularly if you live in an area which hosts special events. Many people who live in and around Henley on Thames, for example, rent out their houses and go away on holiday while the Regatta is on in early July. Similarly, inhabitants of Goodwood, Newmarket and Ascot are able to rent out rooms and houses when the horse racing is on. The fast-approaching Millennium and the associated celebrations in and around Greenwich, for example, have prompted Lewisham and Greenwich councils to encourage local residents to consider renting out rooms on a bed-and-breakfast basis. And many owners of large country houses and stately homes have already started to take bookings for Millennium parties at very lucrative rates.

If you live in a location popular with tourists you may be able to rent out a room or even the house during the tourist season, or even all year round in some cities. Many tourists prefer to stay in a private house than a hotel. However, where do you live while you rent your house? If you are lucky enough to have a self-contained annexe, you could move in there for the duration of the special event. If the event is on for quite a short period (two weeks or less) and you cannot stand the disruption it causes in your normally tranquil town, then you could rent out your home and go on holiday (and still make a profit from the deal).

CASE HISTORY: Lynn and Nigel

Lynn and Nigel were left a house with fairly extensive grounds on the Isle of Wight by an elderly relative. The property also benefited from a bungalow at the bottom of the garden. When they discovered that they could rent out the main house for at least £300 a week during the summer season (and for more just before and during Cowes Week!), they decided to sell their house in Portsmouth and move to the island permanently. They live in the main house during the winter and move into the bungalow in the spring and summer and part of autumn. They find it a very suitable arrangement and the rentals generate a healthy income.

Looking for the right property

Alternatively, you may be thinking about selling up and buying a larger property, either in a rural or seaside area, or anywhere generally cheaper, with a view to setting up a business. What should you be looking for?

First you have to know what kind of business you want to run. Regulations governing the use of buildings, the quality and the standard of the business and many other pertinent regulations are far-reaching and stringent. The following requirements by Kent County Council for two of the most popular business uses of large houses – a residential care home for adults and a day nursery – demonstrate the myriad regulations with which you must comply. They also show that such an undertaking is not to be taken lightly. Failure to comply with regulations results in prosecution.

A residential care home for adults

According to Kent County Council Standards for Registration the proposed premises must be suitable in construction and situation. Registration will not be approved unless applicants show that:

- the use intended is covered by a grant of planning permission
- the building does not contravene building regulations
- Food Act 1984, Food Safety Act 1990, Food Hygiene (General) Regulations and other relevant regulations are complied with
- the building complies with all current fire regulations
- the electrical installation is safe and inspected by a competent contractor. A certificate issued by the inspecting contractor must be available for inspection at the home
- gas or oil appliances, lifts, fire alarms, emergency lighting and other major items are regularly maintained. Certificates must be available for inspection at the home
- there is adequate external amenity space within the site so that residents can take exercise and enjoy fresh air
- there is reasonable access to public transport, shops and other facilities
- there is adequate car parking
- there is full access for emergency vehicles
- there is adequate insurance cover: employer's liability, public liability, premises and contents. Certificates must be available for inspection at the home and premiums must be paid up to date.

There are additional standards on facilities and amenities such as handrails, lifts, lavatories, baths, showers, bedrooms, day rooms, hand basins, telephones, call systems, laundry facilities, storage, types of furniture, temperature of rooms, lighting, windows, adequacy of staffing levels and other matters.

Day nursery/creche/playgroup/nursery school

Under the Children Act 1989 the following regulations apply:

Day care for children aged under two years
- space required 40 square feet per child
- sterile conditions for food
- a kitchen for the preparation of food must be provided and it must be inspected and approved by the Environmental Health Department
- there must be hygienic nappy disposal and potty sterilisation
- staff ratio must be – 1 adult to 3 babies – minimum

Day care for children aged from two to three years
- space required 30 square feet per child
- hygienic nappy disposal and potty sterilisation
- inspected and approved kitchen
- toilets – 1 to 10 children
- staff ratio – 1 adult to 4 children minimum

Day care for children aged three to five
- space required 25 square feet per child
- approved and inspected kitchen
- toilets – 1 to 10 children
- staff ratio 1 adult to 8 children minimum

There may be a maximum of 26 children in one room providing that the space requirements per child as specified in the Act are complied with.

The Social Services department inspectors will have to approve the following items:

- floor covering
- the availability of a sink in the playroom
- sleeping arrangements (for daytime naps)
- buggy storage

- toy storage
- outdoor facilities (either attached or use of public facilities nearby)
- first aid equipment and training
- free milk per day per child
- compliance with fire regulations
- compliance with building regulations
- compliance with health and safety regulations
- compliance with food hygiene regulations
- compliance with the Children Act 1989.

As you can see from all these regulations, undertaking this sort of business in your home is not for the faint-hearted. It would be worthwhile to look for a building which has already been converted for the specific use that you intend.

Less ambitious requirements

Even a hairdresser operating from a small salon in his or her front room is subject to various local bylaws relating to the conditions in which business is conducted. All local authorities will have bylaws under Section 77 of the Public Health Act 1961 which stipulate that all surfaces in the salon – walls, floors, seating, etc., should be in good repair at all times and capable of being washed. Rules govern the disposal of rubbish and the availability of washing facilities, toilet facilities, water supply and cleanliness of utensils.

The regulations are particularly stringent when it comes to services which involve the use of needles such as acupuncture, ear piercing, body piercing and tattooing. Because of the potential public health risks any such operation being conducted from someone's house would be subjected to a mountain of hygiene regulations and frequent inspections.

Any home-based operation which involves the preparation of food is also subject to a battery of regulations. If this is your chosen business, you will obviously be looking for a house with a kitchen of a very high standard.

Even if you were merely intending to run an office-based business from home you need to think about suitability when viewing premises. If you are likely to have clients visiting you, it rather detracts from your company image if they have to go through your kitchen and utility room into a lean-to construction in order to conduct business. On the other hand, if they come into a large double-fronted house and your office is to the right of the front door in the spacious room that once would have been the front parlour, this creates altogether a different image. If you are likely to have business visitors you must consider accessibility and parking. Much as you would love to buy an old chapel in the Welsh hills, if your customers need to visit, they may be put off by the long journey and the inaccessibility of your premises and may even start to look for someone else closer to them with whom to do business. Similarly, if you invest in a town house in a city centre and there is no parking to be had anywhere, customers may be discouraged.

What about your outbuildings?

If you would rather have your house to yourself and not host your own or anyone else's businesses from there, then you could consider renting out your outbuildings.

A dry, warm barn with a power supply can be a great asset – not just for renting out for those occasional barn dances but, perhaps, for something more permanent, as the premises for a small business, for example. Barns in remote places are often just what craftsmen and women and artists may be looking for.

The Rural Development Commission (RDC)* administers Redundant Building Grants which have enabled around 3,900 rural buildings, including old dairies, schoolhouses and chapels, to be converted into productive sources of income for their owners.

Applications to the RDC are considered from individuals, partnerships, limited companies, co-operatives or charitable trusts as either owners or tenants. Tenants must have a fixed-term lease with at least five years left to run and written consent for the proposed works from their landlord.

Grants are normally limited to a maximum of 25 per cent of the total eligible costs of a project. The minimum grant is £2,500. In exceptional circumstances, and where significant extra employment will be created, projects costing more than £60,000 may be considered for grants up to 30 per cent of eligible costs. Funds from other public sector sources should not, together with the Redundant Building Grant, exceed 50 per cent of the total cost of the project.

Application must be made and approved before work starts and grants would normally be paid on completion of the work.

Uses of redundant outbuildings have become quite varied. One expanding business area is the conversion of barns into 'playbarns'. These are children's indoor play areas – multi-level, soft play equipment jungles which allow children to let off steam safely. More and more buildings are being converted to this use (most of the playbarns are franchises) but – be warned – the insurance premiums are very steep and the staff levels have to be high because the Children Act requires that children be carefully supervised, even though all these playbarns state that parents must supervise their own children.

Other popular conversions are little garden centres, tropical fish centres, craft centres, indoor bowling, indoor cricket and small manufacturing units.

CASE HISTORY: Jessica

Jessica is a farmer's widow and she owns a farm of some 100 acres in North Yorkshire. The farm used to raise beef but suffered a decline due to the BSE crisis and the death of Jessica's husband. Jessica has no children and owns the farm outright and does not want to sell it, so she decides to make the land pay for itself in other ways. She sets up a caravan park with her brother-in-law in one of the lower fields. They invest some £30,000 to install amenities – electricity, water – and build some toilet and shower blocks. Jessica decides to run the site shop herself and she employs a local girl to help her. Another field is let out for fairs, shows and markets. Business for this has increased in the past two years and an event is held in that field every month or so. The woodland has been rented out to a local shooting club, mostly wealthy businessmen who like to target shoot in the woods. There is a large wooden barn, which has a preservation order on it. Jessica has decided to renovate it and install heating and other amenities so that it can be rented out for functions. She has applied for planning permission to tarmac part of an adjoining field to use as a car park. She is currently investigating other ways in which she can capitalise on her land and thus never have to move from her home.

On a more modest level you could, of course, rent out any out-buildings, including garages (much sought after in urban areas), greenhouses, sheds and stables – anything, in fact, that you do not use but would be of value to someone else.

When looking at properties with a view to buying them, you should never discount the land and outbuildings. If contemplating a move from town to country, you might feel that any land is too much to cope with and you are never going to use the stables that are in the second field – but someone will – and those outbuildings could bring you in some money. For example, there are over 1,000 farmers who offer hospitality to visitors, either in the farmhouse as bed, breakfast and evening meal, or in cottages or converted farm buildings as self catering. These enterprising farmers are members of the Farm Holiday Bureau,★ which exists to advise members on successful farm tourism. You don't have to be a farmer to develop those outbuildings or derelict cottages into a tourism enterprise.

Making the most of your land assets

What about trees?

Suppose you have a redundant farm or a lot of land which, although it provides a wonderful view, does not actually contribute to the paying of the bills. You could, of course, as many landowners do, rent out fields to farmers, to plant crops or keep livestock, rent to horse, pony and donkey owners, or rent it out for sports to be played. But what about trees?

The Forestry Commission★ awards grants for establishing and looking after woodlands and forests.

The aims of the Woodland Grant Scheme are:

- to encourage people to create new woodlands and forests to
  - increase the production of wood
  - improve the landscape
  - provide new habitats for wildlife and
  - offer opportunities for recreation and sport
- to encourage good management of forests and woodlands, including their well-timed regeneration, particularly looking after the needs of ancient and semi-natural woodlands
- to provide jobs and improve the economy of rural areas and other areas with few other sources of economic activity

- to provide a use for land instead of agriculture.

Grants for the creation of new woodlands (providing your application met all the necessary criteria) are currently as follows:

Rate of grant	Conifers	Broadleaves
Woods less than 10 hectares (ha)	£700 per ha	£1,350 per ha
Woods more than 10 ha	£700 per ha	£1,050 per ha

Grants are paid in two instalments – 70 per cent when planting is finished and 30 per cent after five years. You must maintain the area to the satisfaction of the Forestry Commission for at least ten years.

The Farm Woodland Premium Scheme is designed to enhance the environment through the planting of farm woodlands, in particular to improve the landscape, provide new habitats and increase biodiversity. The scheme offers a variety of payments depending on the size of the proposed woodland, whether or not it is on set-aside land, and other factors.

The Forest Authority (part of the Forestry Commission) takes the planning and management of woodland very seriously. A variety of factors must be considered: the existing land, sources of water, prevailing wildlife, open ground, recreational potential and so on. An information pack is available from the Forestry Commission.

Wind farms

One of the most interesting but also the most controversial uses of redundant farmland in recent years has been the establishment of wind farms. As yet there are relatively few wind farms in the UK, mainly because many local communities have opposed their construction. If you are interested in installing a wind farm on your land contact the British Wind Energy Association.★

Animal establishments

Using land to set up animal-related businesses is very popular, and riding stables and kennels/catteries are the most common choices. If you decide to open a kennels or cattery you will need to apply to your local Environmental Health Department for a licence. If you opt for a riding establishment you will need a licence from your local authority. Remember that the regulations covering such licences will be strict.

Caravan sites

Caravan sites need to be licensed by the local authority and, in most cases, require planning permission. You may not require planning permission for a seasonal touring caravan site but you most certainly will for a permanent residential site or a site where you own the caravans, which are permanently on site and you rent them out to the public.

A caravan site, of any kind, must have a satisfactory main water supply, waste water disposal, sewage disposal, refuse disposal, sufficient and satisfactory fire-fighting appliances, safe storage facilities for liquified petroleum gas, fully inspected electricity supply and adequate toilet and washing facilities.

Location for TV and film

If you think that your property's greatest asset is that it is beautiful, ancient, unusual, remote, tiny, vast – in other words just extraordinary, then it may be worth compiling a portfolio of photographs of your home and/or garden and sending it to several film and television production companies for consideration as a location. Interiors are just as sought after as exteriors; you may have original wood panelling and beams in your home that would make a wonderful background shot for some TV drama. Sometimes a piece of land, without the modern eyesores of pylons, aircraft, telephone poles and tarmac road is what a location company is looking for, on which to shoot a period drama. Most television and film companies do not advertise for locations but hire a Locations Manager for each production, whose job it is to find the right location. The BBC has a Locations Department and there are one or two specialist location agencies including Lavish Locations★ and Location Works.★ *The Broadcasting Blue Book* contains the names and addresses of most of these agencies. Location work can be lucrative, but it is also a tremendous upheaval to your life, with film crews swarming all over the place at all kinds of hours.

With some careful preparation and knowledge of and compliance with local authority bylaws and regulations it is possible to make your bricks and mortar, grass and paddock work for you. It will not be easy and the rewards may be a long time in coming but more often than not the benefits outweigh the disadvantages.

Chapter 13

Employing others

The time will finally come, if you are successful and the business takes off, when you have to expand your operation and employ someone else. Of course, you may already have planned this from the beginning as a family venture, always intending that your home should be the centre of you and your family's livelihood. It may be that your home is the business – you take paying guests, you grow crops on the land, you rent your outbuildings as workshops and so on – and therefore it has been a family venture from the start.

For others, however, who may have been enjoying the luxury (for it is a luxury) of working for themselves and by themselves in their own home, the trauma of having to become an employer can be considerable, particularly if you want to continue to be based in your home. If you have been working for the last year in the converted spare bedroom, which makes a very nice office/craft room/workshop/despatch room but only has enough space for you, what are you going to do about housing another working person? After all, it may be that you chose your current occupation precisely because it would allow you to work at home and to have to move out and set up an office/workshop somewhere else would defeat the object of the whole exercise and add considerably to costs.

Apart from the practicalities, you should consider the personal issues. You have got used to being on your own, working to your own routine, not having to think about anyone else, or explain what needs doing. You may have to give up working irregular hours in order to supervise an employee who works 'normal' hours. Of course, you may be working 24 hours a day and desperately need help but that may not make the prospect of sharing your space, particularly in your own home, with someone else any easier. If the thought of it truly depresses you, then think about the options.

Carry on as you are

This is probably not an option unless you are the second-income generator and you are able to make an easy decision not to expand your activities. If you just want a paying hobby, some spare money in retirement or an enjoyable but reasonably lucrative pastime, you can carry on in your splendid isolation and not worry about finding the right sort of staff.

If your family is relying on the money you earn from home, however, you may have no option but to get some help. You do not necessarily have to appoint a permanent employee – becoming an employer is something that you can do in easy stages.

Involve your family more

You may be able to employ your wife, husband, son, daughter, mother, father, anyone in the family who has the time, the interest and the capabilities to do some work for you. At least you know each other and it is not like having a stranger coming to work in your home. You should be able to trust members of your family to

---

CASE HISTORY: Christina

Christina is a freelance public relations consultant. She found that using an office services bureau and an answerphone was just not enough to give her the required amount of credibility with clients. She was having difficulty finding the right person to handle all her secretarial work when her widowed mother suggested stepping in to fill the post temporarily. Christina's mother had assisted her father in his business activities all her life. After working for her daughter for two months it was apparent that the arrangement worked so well that she is now employed full-time as her daughter's secretary.

---

do their best for you and the situation should be considerably more relaxed than that of traditional employer/employee.

There are dangers, though, in employing family members. For a start, it is most certainly not the way to shore up a crumbling marriage. If a relationship is already under stress, the added strain of the uncertainties of self-employment and the unnatural situation of you and your spouse trying to be employer and employee will undoubtedly drive the final nail into the coffin.

There may be the temptation of employing your teenage children because they are having difficulty getting a job elsewhere. This is a mistake unless they are genuinely interested in your business. There is nothing worse than employing sullen offspring who resent the fact that they have been railroaded into a career in which they are not interested and are expected to be grateful to boot. It is a 'no-win' situation. You end up by becoming more and more frustrated with each other, each feeling obliged to stick it out because it is 'family'.

Employing one or other parent could be just as stressful. Most parents and most adult 'children' would not be able to handle the role reversal of the child employing the parent and telling him or her what to do. However, if you have a good relationship with your parents and one or other is capable of acting as your secretary, accountant, or 'other pair of hands', then make the most of it.

Employ friends

Think about this very carefully before you do it. Employing a friend can be the quickest way to say goodbye to a great friendship. Friends who become employees can often resent the suddenly formal nature of the working relationship. Friends who become employers are disappointed that the friend with whom they thought they had so much in common does not view the business with the same degree of importance as they do.

The only way that a friendship might endure through a working situation is if the two of you became equal partners in a venture at the outset. It certainly would not work if you, having worked alone for a year or more, then took your friend on as a partner. The relationship and partnership would never survive your inability to adapt from working alone and making all the decisions to sharing everything.

Use a bureau

This is probably the best option for the self-employed person who is cautiously expanding. An office services bureau can be your secretary, receptionist, book-keeper, mailroom and more, all rolled into one. If you have one conveniently close to your home (look in the *Yellow Pages*) even better. It is simple for you to drop off work and pick it up the next day, although it still requires you to be highly organised, since you need to plan the daily/weekly work for the bureau.

A good bureau can offer a variety of useful services: typing (audio, copy, word processing), data processing, addressing labels and filling envelopes for mailshots, printing, binding reports, desktop publishing, receiving and sending faxes, being an answering service and so on.

Hire a temp occasionally

If you have a situation where paperwork gets on top of you now and then, you could hire a temporary secretary from time to time from an employment or recruitment agency. This is less daunting than taking on someone full-time as you know you are only going to be employing that person for a short period. It is a good way of gradually getting used to being an employer and, indeed, having someone working alongside you.

Subcontract

Subcontracting is a common way of dealing with sudden overloads of work in certain trades, like building and clothing. It is always worth 'networking' with other people in your area who have similar skills; it lays the foundations of a good working relationship so that, at some point, you can approach someone and subcontract certain parts of your work to them. This is discussed in Chapter 4.

CASE HISTORY: Daniella

Daniella designs and hand-prints fabrics and makes clothing from them. She got a very large order from a chain of fashion stores and decided she could not cope alone. She rang round all of the people she had been at college with and found that three of them were still looking for work. She could not afford to employ them but she offered them subcontract work. She rented machines for them and then supplied the printed fabric and a copy of the clothing pattern. Her subcontractors then cut and sewed the garments on her behalf. She could not have used outworkers because she needed skilled designers/cutters like herself to be able to duplicate her work exactly.

Use outworkers

If you want to continue to use your own home as a base but do not want any employees working from there and you also do not want or cannot afford to rent an office, warehouse or factory, taking on outworkers may be one solution. You can use outworkers (see Chapter 3) as long as it is practical and it complies with any relevant regulations. There are some situations where it would not be feasible – for example, if you made cakes for a living and you were swamped with orders, you could get outworkers to bake cakes for you but unless their kitchens were of the standard required by the Environmental Health Department, you would have to have the outworkers bake in your own kitchen.

Most employers, certainly those just starting out, prefer outworkers to be self-employed so that the employer does not have to get involved in National Insurance and tax. If you pay an outworker less than £64 per week (1998/9 rates), there is no liability for National Insurance for you or your outworker. But, strictly speaking, outworkers can be classed as self-employed only if they satisfy certain criteria (see Chapter 6). Also, the Inland Revenue may not regard anyone as self-employed who has no real management over their own work.

Finding suitable workers for your line of business may not be easy. You may make clothing and know plenty of people who sew but who are not skilled machinists with experience of making clothing or parts of clothing to exacting commercial specifications. You may have to advertise or go through a JobCentre to get some staff.

If any special equipment is needed you should, as the employer, provide it. You will also have to insure it, making sure that it is fully covered even though it is not on your premises, and maintain it so that it meets the legal safety requirements. You may also have to spend some time at the outset training your outworkers to deal with the equipment you have provided for them.

Finding efficient and reliable workers is a matter of trial and error. One of the drawbacks of outworkers is that you are not there to supervise them and, although you are probably paying them by results (so much per unit completed or per hundred), you have no guarantee that this will be enough of an incentive to make them work hard for you. You could insist on a probationary period of, say, three months and see whether things work out. The majority of outworkers work from home because they are tied to the home through disability, illness or a family. Therefore all sorts of things can happen such as a period of worse health, children falling ill, school holidays and family demands in general which affect the quantity of work and, possibly, the quality. You have to be able to assess whether each outworker is giving you what you need in the end.

It takes some time for a team of outworkers to be trained and to settle down into an efficient working unit. For this reason you should not rush to use unknown outworkers just to see you through a particularly busy patch.

Take a partner who also works from home

This kind of arrangement works particularly well if you have complementary but not identical skills – that way you both feel that you are not being submerged by the other and you both bring something different and valuable to the business. It is a way of expanding and diversifying without actually becoming an employer. It is especially suited to consultants, who spend a lot of their working week away from their 'desks' and might meet up once a week to discuss developments. It is also suitable for craftsmen and women, who often prefer to work alone in their workshops. Two carpenters might join forces in this way, one making tables and chairs, the other making cabinets and drawers. It could be a permanent partnership or a joint venture just for a specific project. Either way, a clear contract is essential if disputes are to be avoided.

CASE HISTORY: Imran

Imran runs his own computer services bureau from home. His particular interest is in designing programs, software training and dealing with computer viruses. However, as he was increasingly being asked if he provided technical maintenance and repair for the hardware, he decided to find a partner who would handle this. He advertised in various computer magazines and eventually found Richard. They both operate from their own homes but under the same company name. Imran's wife continues to make appointments with clients. She then rings Richard and Imran to tell them where their next jobs are. Most of the time they work in different places on different projects.

Take on an apprentice

If you do not need to work alone and you enjoy explaining and teaching your work to others, you could consider taking on an apprentice or trainee. You may be able to send your apprentice on a government training scheme. Consult your local Training and Enterprise Council (TEC) or Local Enterprise Company (LEC) in Scotland for further information.

Your trainee/apprentice does not have to be a school-leaver. The government also encourages older men and women, particularly in former coal and steel areas, to retrain for employment, and many early retirers are looking for a new direction in life and would willingly sign up as an apprentice. Taking on an apprentice/trainee should never be considered as a form of cheap labour – that sort of attitude will do nothing but harm to the working relationship between you and your helper. If the person has promise and could shape up into the ideal employee or eventual partner, you want to do everything to make sure that you keep him or her. This means being fair in all ways – working practices, quality of training and money.

Taking on your first employee

Before you try to find your employee you have to decide exactly what you want that person to do and be very clear about it. What will be his or her duties and responsibilities? Does the job require any qualifications? Do you require the employee to drive? Are keyboard skills essential? Do you want him or her to develop a new part of the business or clear up the mess in the paperwork caused by you struggling alone? A candidate who applies for a position with you expecting it to be one thing and finding that it is another will be very resentful. For example, if you run a catering business from your home, the applicant who hopes for 'hands-on' catering work is going to be disappointed if you do not make it plain that you are looking for a secretary and not a fellow chef.

Another consideration is personality. Will your employee be required to deal with the public? If so, an outgoing and pleasant nature is essential. You do not want to end up with complaints from customers about the surly treatment they received from your staff. If he or she is going to be working with you all day and you are a bit of a loner, you will want someone quieter and more reserved. Does appearance matter in your line of work? Will your employee be representing your business to the outside world? Will your customers expect a certain dress code? Think carefully about such matters before you hire your staff.

When you advertise the job, whether through a publication, shop window, JobCentre, employment agency or in a school or college, you need to put in as much information about the job and your requirements as possible. You may not, by law, state a preference for anyone of a particular gender, religion, ethnic background or physical ability in your advertisement, nor should you discriminate when the applicants come forward.

When you receive the applications, take note of their presentation if this is relevant to the job. There is no point in interviewing someone as a potential secretary if he or she has untidy handwriting or sloppy typing and cannot spell or punctuate. If you are hiring someone for their specialist skills you need to see examples of their work. You can also make the job offer subject to the receipt of satisfactory references. Always take up references. Employees' and employers' rights and regulations are covered in detail in *The Which? Guide to Employment*.

Contracts of employment

All employees, whether full- or part-time, are entitled to a written statement of particulars of employment. This lays down the terms and conditions of the job in question and cannot be changed by either party without adequate consultation. The statement should be given to an employee within two months of commencement of employment. It is advisable for the employee to see the terms and conditions of employment as a whole prior to accepting employment.

The written statement of particulars must include the following:

- full names of both parties
- job title
- date the employment will start and, if the employee is hired for a specific period, the date the employment will finish
- place of work
- rate and frequency of pay
- hours of work
- holiday entitlement – amount to be taken and if with pay
- notice period
- sick pay details
- pension arrangements
- disciplinary procedures.

You may wish to include additional important matters in the contract, such as a confidentiality clause (that is, your employee must not disclose any of your or your clients' business information to any other party). An employee may wish to negotiate over his or her terms of employment, so do not necessarily expect the first draft of the contract to be the final one.

ACAS (the Advisory, Conciliation and Arbitration Service)★ will give free advice on drawing up contracts of employment.

Employment law

Employees are entitled to Statutory Sick Pay (SSP) if they are ill for more than three consecutive days and have worked for you for three months continuously and made adequate NI contributions. In 1998–9 the maximum weekly amount is £57.70. As an employer you pay the SSP to your employee and this is no longer an expense which can be recovered, unfortunately, unless you have several staff who are ill and you experience a large degree of absenteeism, then you qualify under the Percentage Threshold Scheme to recover some of the SSP paid out during a certain period. You need to take advice from your local Contributions Agency because the rules on SSP are complicated. A booklet, *Recovering Statutory Sick Pay*, gives a detailed explanation of the system and is available from the Benefits Agency.★

An employee is eligible to receive Statutory Maternity Pay (SMP) from her employer if she has been continuously employed by that employer for at least 26 weeks by the 15th week before her Expected Week of Confinement (EWC) and her average weekly earning are on, or above, the lower earnings limit for the purpose of NI contributions (£64 in 1998). As an employer you are obliged to keep a woman's job open for her after she has given birth. In the case of small employers with five or less employees, there is no obligation to allow the employee to return to work after the period of extended maternity leave (up to 29 weeks after the birth) if it is not reasonably practicable to keep her job open. Pregnant women are entitled to be paid for the time they have to take off to attend an ante-natal clinic and certain medically prescribed antenatal classes.

Employees are entitled to an itemised pay statement at appointed intervals showing gross pay, variable deductions (e.g. income tax, NI) and other agreed deductions (e.g. pensions), then the total net pay after deductions (and where parts of the net figure are paid differently, the amount and method of each part-payment).

Employees are also entitled to a minimum period of notice as follows:

Service	Notice entitlement
1 month – 2 years	1 week
2 years	2 weeks
3 years and so on	3 weeks
12 or more	12 weeks maximum

However, it may have been agreed in the contract of employment that the minimum period of notice will be longer than the statutory minimum.

An employee can claim wrongful dismissal if he or she is dismissed without notice or justification. The employee's starting point for claiming compensation in such circumstances is the sum equal to the value of the net salary and fringe benefits which he or she would have received during the notice period. The compensation claim will be reduced if he or she gets another job within the notice period. In which case any earnings received during the notice period will be taken into account in assessing the compensation due.

An employer should follow an agreed disciplinary procedure before dismissing an employee. ACAS provides guidelines of the procedures that should be included in any employer's disciplinary procedure. For more information, employers can consult *Discipline at Work*, an advisory handbook from ACAS.

Failure by the employer to follow such a procedure can result in the employee, if he or she has been in the same employment for over two years, presenting a claim for unfair dismissal to an employment tribunal and asking for compensation. At present this compensation is limited to a compensatory award of a maximum of £12,000 plus a basic award calculated in the same way as the statutory redundancy payment (see below). There is also a claim called constructive dismissal, which can be brought by employees who, as a result of their employer's serious breach of contract, resign and treat themselves as having been dismissed without notice or justification. In these circumstances the employee may claim for wrongful dismissal and, if eligible, unfair dismissal.

If an employee is dismissed by reason of redundancy the dismissal procedure should be carefully handled. If the employee is dismissed without notice or justification he or she will have a claim for wrongful dismissal. If the employee has the necessary period of qualifying service and is declared redundant he or she may have a claim for unfair dismissal. An employee is generally speaking redundant when the employer has a requirement for fewer employees to carry out a particular job. An employee may have a claim for unfair dismissal if he or she can show the position is not redundant or he or she was unfairly selected or the employer failed to consult adequately with him or her before making the redundancy decision.

Employers may find it useful to consult a leaflet entitled *Fair and Unfair Dismissal: A Guide for Employers* (PL714), available from the DTI Publications Orderline.★

Redundant employees may claim a tax-free statutory redundancy payment provided they have the appropriate qualifying period of employment. The statutory amount for employees aged over 18 or under normal retirement age is as follows:

- for each year of service from the age of 18 up to the age of 21 the employee receives half of one week's pay
- for each year of service between the ages of 21 and 41 inclusive, the employee receives one week's pay
- for each year of service between the ages of 42 and 64 inclusive, the employee receives one and a half week's pay.

For the purposes of calculating the statutory redundancy payment a week's pay is currently fixed at £220.

The Which? Guide to Employment covers redundancy and dismissal procedures in depth.

Tax and National Insurance

All the information and the necessary forms for first-time employers can be found in the Inland Revenue's *New Employer's Starter Pack*.

You need to contact your PAYE tax office (which may be different from the tax office that deals with your business) and fill in a form to tell them that you have now employed someone. Each pay-day you must work out the tax and National Insurance charges due with the help of a set of tax and NI tables given to you by the PAYE tax office. The deductions you make from your employee's pay are then paid over to the PAYE tax office every month. At the end of the year you have to do a summary which tells the tax office how much each employee has earned and how much tax and National Insurance you have deducted.

That is the *basic* system. There are, of course, forms to fill in and the Inland Revenue will have to give you PAYE codes for each employee which show how much the individual employee's tax allowances amount to. But the Inland Revenue tries to be as helpful as possible to new employers and will talk you through the system if you wish.

Self-assessment is the new tax system and a new employer cannot do better than obtain the *Guide to Self-Assessment Pack for Employers*, available from the Inland Revenue. It contains booklets, sample forms and a cassette tape to give you all the advice you need. Also any Inland Revenue inspector will give you free advice and time to help you administer the system.

Keeping employees

Once you have them and you are happy with them, you want to keep them, and this requires more than a little effort on your part. Everyone appreciates being told if they are:

* doing a good job
* behaving responsibly
* learning the ropes quickly and thoroughly
* being a great help to you
* helping the business to develop.

You must make time to assess your employees' development and to guide them if they have difficulty learning particular skills or dealing with certain tasks.

If you have one treasured employee or a small team of excellent workers, consider rewarding them. It does not have to be cash bonuses – it could just be an outing that you pay for, perhaps a meal or a visit to the theatre.

Make any criticisms of staff constructive. Never lose your temper – it is not productive. If you are plunged into a crisis do not waste time trying to apportion blame; direct your energies instead to overcoming the crisis, then, when it has all died down, institute a quiet investigation into what went wrong. Never humiliate a member of staff in front of his or her colleagues as you will lose everybody's respect that way. If you have a bone to pick with someone take them away quietly for a private chat.

If you can, make your employees' work interesting. It is not always possible in the case of outworkers doing mundane, repetitive jobs, of course. In that case, try to be fair about money and understand that, if your profit margins can bear it, people need to be rewarded for doing difficult, unfulfilling jobs.

Listen to your employees. Some of the best money-making ideas have come from members of staff. Also heed what they have to say about procedures and routines within your business. You may have done it your way for such a long time you cannot see the wood for the trees. A fresh mind applies itself to the job and suddenly certain flaws in the system become apparent.

Do not be jealous of a new employee. That sounds a silly thing to say but it is a common feeling among lone entrepreneurs who have nursed their 'baby' from concept to profitability. The first employee may be full of eagerness and new ideas and the employer initially may resent any 'interference'.

Above all, communicate with your employees. Tell them how the business is doing, explain any problems, reassure them about future orders and contracts, explain your philosophy and your hopes. This is very important if you have just one employee who, perhaps, stands in for you when you are not there. He or she needs to be able to think as you do, to deal with any problems or exploit any opportunities that may arise while you are away. While you do not want to give an employee the impression that he or she can make important decisions without referring to you, you do want someone who will take a bit of responsibility and initiative in your absence.

Human relationships are a tricky business at the best of times. Just remember that being an employer does not make you a different person from the one who started out earning money from home in a very modest way. If a particular association, whether with employee, colleague or client, fails to work out, accept the situation and end the relationship as simply as you can.

Addresses

All those organisations, associations and government offices marked with an asterisk in the text are listed below. Your local reference library will have information on associations for specific lines of work and regional bodies which are too numerous to mention here.

ACAS
(Advisory, Conciliation and
Arbitration Service)
London, Eastern and Southern Area
Office
Clifton House
83–117 Euston Road
London NW1 2RB
Tel: 0171 396 5100
Fax: 0171 396 5159
Web site: www.acas.org.uk

ADAS
(Food, farming, land and leisure
consultancy)
Headquarters:
Oxford Spires Business Park
The Boulevard
Kidlington
Oxon OX5 1NZ
Tel: (01865) 842742
Fax: (01865) 845055
Web site: www.adas.co.uk

Advertising Standards Authority
Brook House
2 Torrington Place
London WC1E 7HW
Tel: 0171 580 5555
Fax: 0171 631 3051
Web site: www.asa.org.uk

Arts Council of England
14 Great Peter Street
London SW1P 3NQ
Tel: 0171 333 0100
Fax: 0171 973 6590
Web site: www.arts.council.org.uk

Association of British Insurers
51 Gresham Street
London EC2V 7HQ
Tel: 0171 600 3333
Fax: 0171 696 8999
Web site: www.abi.org.uk

Banking Ombusman
70 Gray's Inn Road
London WC1X 8NB
Tel: (0345) 660902
Fax: 0171 405 5052
Web site: www.obo.org.uk

British Agents Register
24 Mount Parade
Harrogate
N Yorks HG1 1BP
Tel: (01423) 560608
Fax: (01423) 561204

British Chambers of Commerce
Manning House
22 Carlisle Place
London SW1P 1JA
Tel: 0171 565 2000
Fax: 0171 565 2049

British Franchise Association
Thames View
Newtown Road
Henley-on-Thames
Oxon RG9 1HG
Tel: (01491) 578050
Fax: (01491) 573517
Email: mailroom@british-franchise.org.uk
Web site: www.british-franchise.org.uk

British Overseas Trade Board (BOTB)
Department of Trade and Industry
Kingsgate House
66–74 Victoria Street
London SW1E 6SW
Tel: 0171 215 5000
Fax: 0171 215 4598

British Standards Institution
389 Chiswick High Road
London W4 4AL
Tel: 0181 996 9000
Fax: 0181 996 7400
Web site: www.bsi.org.uk

British Wind Energy Association
42 Kingsway
London WC2B 6EX
Tel: 0171 402 7102
Web site: www.bwea.com

Building Societies Ombudsman
Millbank Tower
Millbank
London SW1P 4XS
Tel: 0171 931 0044
Fax: 0171 931 8485
E-mail:
blgsocombudsman@easynet.co.uk

Business Connect (Wales)
Tel: 0345 969798

Business Link Signpost Line
Tel: (0345) 567765
240 Business Links open throughout England

Central Office of Information
Commercial Publicity
Hercules House
Hercules Road
London SE1 7DU
Tel: 0171 261 8422
Fax: 0171 928 9034

Chartered Institute of Patent Agents
Staple Inn Buildings
High Holborn
London WC1V 7PZ
Tel: 0171 405 9450
Fax: 0171 430 0471
Email: mail@cipa.org.uk
Web site: www.cipa.org.uk

Companies House (England and Wales)
Crown Way
Maindy
Cardiff
South Glamorgan CF4 3UZ
Tel: 01222 380801
Fax: 01222 380900
Email:
nbarnes@companieshouse.gov.uk
Web site:
www.companieshouse.gov.uk

Companies House (Scotland)
37 Castle Terrace
Edinburgh EH1 2EB
Tel: 0131 535 5800
Fax: 0131 535 5820
Web site:
www.companieshouse.gov.uk

Companies Registry (Northern Ireland)
IDB House
64 Chichester Street
Belfast BT1 4JX
Tel: 01232 234488
Fax: 01232 544888

Consumers' Association
2 Marylebone Road
London NW1 4DF
Tel: 0171 830 6000
Fax: 0171 830 6220
Email: books@which.net
Web site: www.which.net

Which? Legal Service, offering help and advice on problems with goods or services, is available for £9.75 a quarter
Tel: 0800 252100

Crafts Council
44A Pentonville Road
London N1 9BY
Tel: 0171 278 7700
Fax: 0171 837 6891
Email:
reference@craftscouncil.org.uk
Web site: www.craftscouncil.org.uk

HM Customs and Excise
Dorset House
Stamford Street
London SE1 9PY
Tel: 0171 928 3344
Fax: 0171 202 4131
(or local offices can help)

Data Protection Registrar
Wycliffe House
Water Lane
Wilmslow
Cheshire SK9 5AF
Tel: (01625) 545745
Fax: (01625) 524510
Email: data@wycliffe.demon.co.uk
Web site:
www.open.gov.uk/dpr/dprhome.htm

Department for Education and Employment
Sanctuary Buildings
Great Smith Street
London SW1P 3BT
Tel: 0171 925 5000
Fax: 0171 925 6000
Email: info@dfee.gov.uk
Web site:
www.open.gov.uk/dfee/dfeehome.htm

Department of the Environment, Transport and the Regions
(Public Enquiry Unit)
123 Victoria Street
London SW1E 5DU
Tel: 0171 276 3000
Fax: 0171 890 3000
Web site: www.detr.gov.uk/

Department of Trade and Industry
1 Victoria Street
London SW1H 0ET
Tel: 0171 215 5000
Fax: 0171 222 0612
Email:
dti.enquiries@imsv.dti.gov.uk
Web site: www.dti.gov.uk

DTI Publications Orderline
Admail 528
London SW1W 8YT
Tel: (0870) 1502500
Fax: (0870) 1502333
Email: dtipubs@echristian.co.uk
Web site: www.dti.gov.uk

Direct Mail Information Service
c/o HBH Partnership
5 Carlisle Street
London W1V 6JX
Tel: 0171 494 0483
Fax: 0171 494 0455
Email: jo.harrod-brown@virgin.net
Web site: www.dmis.co.uk

Direct Mail Accreditation Recognition Centre (DMARC)
5th Floor
Haymarket House
1 Oxendon Street
London SW1Y 4EE
Tel: 0171 766 4430
Fax: 0171 976 1886

Direct Marketing Association
Haymarket House
1 Oxendon Street
London SW1Y 4EE
Tel: 0171 321 2525
Fax: 0171 321 0191
Email: dma@dma.org.uk
Web site: www.dma.org.uk

Direct Selling Association (DSA)
6 Carriage Hall
29 Floral Street
London WC2E 9DP
Tel: 0171 497 1234
Fax: 0171 497 3144
Web site: www.dsa.org.uk

The Disability Alliance (ERA)
Universal House
88–94 Wentworth Street
London E1 7SA
Tel: 0171 247 8776
Fax: 0171 247 8765
(Welfare Rights Advice Line 0171 247
8763 Mon & Wed 2pm-4pm only)
Email: da@dial.pipex.com

English Tourist Board
Thames Tower
Black's Road
Hammersmith
London W6 9EL
Tel: 0181 846 9000
Fax: 0181 563 0302
Email:
101657.335@compuserve.com
Web site: www.visitbritain.com

Enterprise Agencies see National
Federation of Enterprise Agencies

Export Market Research Scheme
Tel: (01203) 694492

Europe Information Centres
Tel: (0800) 7836553

Farm Holiday Bureau (UK) Ltd
National Agricultural Centre
Stoneleigh Park
Kenilworth
Warwickshire CV8 2LZ
Tel: (01203) 696909
Fax: (01203) 696630
Email:
admin@fhbaccom.demon.co.uk
Web site: www.webscape.co.uk/far-maccom/

Finance and Leasing Association
Imperial House
15-19 Kingsway
London WC2B 6UN
Tel: 0171 836 6511
Fax: 0171 420 9600
Email: info@fla.org.uk

Food from Britain
123 Buckingham Palace Road
London SW1W 9FA
Tel: 0171 233 5111
Fax: 0171 233 9515

Forestry Commission
231 Corstophine Road
Edinburgh EH12 7AT
Tel: 0131 334 0303
Fax: 0131 334 3047
Email: enquiries@forestry.gov.uk
Web site: www.forestry.gov.uk

Guild of Disabled Homeworkers
Market Street
Nailsworth
Glos GL6 0BX
Tel/Fax: (01453) 835623

Highlands and Islands Enterprise
Bridge House
20 Bridge Street
Inverness IV1 1QR
Tel: (01463) 234171
Fax: (01463) 244469
Email: hie.general@hient.co.uk
Web site: www.hie.co.uk

Inland Revenue
Somerset House
The Strand
London WC2R 1LB
Tel: 0171 438 6622
Tax enquiry line: 0171 438 6420
Web site:
www.inlandrevenue.gov.uk

**Inland Revenue Self-assessment
Orderline**
PO Box 37
St Austell
Cornwall PL25 5YN
Tel: (0645) 000404
Fax: (0645) 000604
Email: saorderline.ir@gtnet.gov.uk
Web site:
www.inlandrevenue.gov.uk
For Inland Revenue helpsheets and leaflets

Institute of Directors
116 Pall Mall
London SW1Y 5ED
Tel: 0171 839 1233
Fax: 0171 930 1949

Institute of Management
Management House
Cottingham Road
Corby
Northants NN17 1TT
Tel: (01536) 204222
Fax: 01536 201651
Email: mie.enquiries@imgt.org.uk
Web site: www.inst-mgt.org.uk

Lavish Locations
Chiswick Town Hall
Heathfield Terrace
London W4 4JN
Tel: 0181 742 2992
Email: Lavish@axiom.co.uk

Livewire
FREEPOST
Newcastle-upon-Tyne
Tyne & Wear NE1 1BR
Tel: 0191 261 5584
Fax: 0191 261 1910
Email: livewire@projectne.co.uk
Web site: www.shel-livewire.org.uk

Location Works
42 Old Compton Street
London W1V 6LR
Tel: 0171 494 0888
Email: info@locationworks.com
Web site: www.locationworks.com

Mail Order Traders Association
40 Waterloo Road
Birkdale
Southport PR8 2NG
Tel: (01704) 563787
Fax: (01704) 551247

Manufacturers Agents Association (MAA)
1 Somers Road
Reigate
Surrey RH2 9DU
Tel: (01737) 241025
Fax: (01737) 2245537

Market Research Society
15 Northburgh Street
London EC1V 0AH
Tel: 0171 490 4911
Fax: 0171 490 0608
Web site:
www.marketresearch.org.uk

Ministry of Agriculture, Fisheries and Food (MAFF)
Whitehall Place
London SW1A 2HH
Helpline: 0645 335577
Fax: 0171 270 8125
Email: helpline@inf.maff.gov.uk
Web site:
www.maff.gov.uk/maffhome.htm

National Association of Teleworkers
The Island House
Midsomer Norton
Bath BA3 2HL
Tel: (01761) 413869
Fax: (01761) 419348

National Farmers Union
164 Shaftesbury Avenue
London WC2H 8HL
Tel: 0171 331 7200
Fax: 0171 331 7313
Email:
nfu.central.services@nfu.org.uk
Web site: www.nfu.org.uk

National Federation of Enterprise Agencies
Trinity Gardens
9–11 Bromham Road
Bedford MK40 2UQ
Tel/Fax: (01234) 354055
Email: alan.bretherton@virgin.net
Web site: www.pne.org/cobweb/nfea

National Federation for Self-Employed and Small Businesses
32 Orchard Road
Lytham St Annes
Lancs FY8 1NY
Tel: (01253) 720911
Fax: (01253) 714651
Email: ho@fsb.org.uk
Web site: www.fsb.org.uk

National Group on Homeworking
Office 26
30-38 Dock Street
Leeds LS10 1JF
Tel: 0113 245 4273
Fax: 0113 246 5616
Email: homeworking@gn.apc.org.uk

National Newspapers Mail Order Protection Scheme (MOPS)
16 Tooks Court
London EC4A 1LB
Tel: 0171 405 6806
Fax: 0171 404 0106
Web site: www.mops.org.uk

Newspaper Society
74–77 Great Russell Street
London WC1B 3DA
Tel: 0171 636 7014
Fax: 0171 631 5119
Email: ns@newspapersoc.org.uk

Office of Fair Trading
Field House
15-25 Bream Buildings
London EC4A 1PR
Tel: 0171 211 8000
Fax: 0171 211 8800
Email: enquiries@oft.gov.uk
Web site: www.oft.gov.uk

Patent Office
Concept House
Cardiff Road
Newport
South Wales NP9 1RH
Tel: (01633) 814000
Fax: (01633) 814444
Web site: www.patent.gov.uk

Princes Trust
18 Park Square East
London NW1 4LH
Tel: 0171 543 1234
Fax: 0171 543 1200
Email: printrust@princes-trust.org.uk
Website: www.princes-trust.org.uk

Remploy Ltd
415 Edgware Road
London NW2 6LR
Tel: 0181 235 0500
Fax: 0181 235 0501

Royal Association for Disability and Rehabilitation (RADAR)
12 City Forum
250 City Road
London EC1V 8AF
Tel: 0171 250 3222
Fax: 0171 250 0212
Email: radar@radar.org.uk
Web site: www.radar.org.uk

Rural Development Commission
141 Castle Street
Salisbury
Wilts SP1 3TP
Tel: (01722) 336255
Fax: (01722) 332769

Scottish Arts Council
12 Manor Place
Edinburgh EH3 7DD
Tel: 0131 226 6051
Fax: 0131 225 9833

Scottish Enterprise
120 Bothwell Street
Glasgow G2 7JP
Tel: 0141 248 2700
Fax: 0141 221 3217
Email: scotentcsd@scotent.co.uk
Web site: www.scotent.co.uk

Scottish Organic Producers
Association (SOPA)
Milton of Cambus Farm
Doune
Perthshire
FK16 6HG
Tel: 01786 841657
Fax: 01786 841455

Scottish Tourist Board
23 Ravelston Terrace
Edinburgh EH4 3EU
Tel: 0131 332 2433
Fax: 0131 343 1513
Web site: www.holiday.scotland.net

Soil Association
Bristol House
40-56 Victoria Street
Bristol
Avon BS1 6BY
Tel: 0117 929 0661
Fax: 0117 925 2504
Email: info@soilassociation.org.uk

The Teaching Company Directorate
Hillside House
79 London Street
Farringdon
Oxon SN7 8AA
Tel: (01367) 242822
Fax: (01367) 242831
Email: office@tcd.co.uk

TCA
Telework, Telecottage and
Telecentre Association
Tel: 0800 616008
Email:
teleworker@compuserve.com
Website: www.tca.org.uk
WREN Telecottage
Stoneleigh Park
Warwickshire CV8 2RR
Tel: (01203) 696986
Fax: (01203) 696 538
Email: wren@ruralnet.org.uk
Web site: www.nrec.org.uk/wren/

TEC National Council
Information line: 0171 735 0010
Web site: www.tec.co.uk

United Kingdom Register of Organic
Food Standards (UKROFS)
c/o MAFF
Room G43
Nobel House
17 Smith Square
London SW1P 3JR
Tel: 0171 238 5915
Fax: 0171 2386148
Web site:
www.maff.gov.uk/environ/envsch/oa
s.htm

Wales Tourist Board
Brunel House
2 Fitzalan Road
Cardiff
South Glamorgan CF2 1UY
Tel: (01222) 499909
Fax: (01222) 485031
Email: info@tourism.wales.gov.uk
Web site: www.visitwales.com

Welsh Arts Council
Holst House
9 Museum Place
Cardiff
South Glamorgan CF1 3NX
Tel: (01222) 276500
Fax: (01222) 221447
Email: information@ccc.acw.org.uk
Web site: www.ccc-acw.org.uk

WI (Women's Institute) Country
Markets Ltd
Reada Court
Vachel Road
Reading RG1 1NY
Tel: 0118 939 4646
Fax: 0118 939 4747

Index

ЙЙ

The Which? Guide to Computers for Small Businesses

Whether you run a small company or simply work at home, this 'pocket consultant' guide will show you how to make the most of your computer system. How do you use your computer to produce professional-looking documents, make VAT and income tax calculations, create promotions and advertising, connect with other computers to share information, keep track of sales and client records, exploit the Internet's potential for increasing business, and deal with the 'Millennium Bug'? *The Which? Guide to Computers for Small Businesses* answers all these questions and many more in simple, non-technical language. The handbook also includes a hardware and software reference section, guidance for buying portable computers, and a glossary of technical and advertising terms.

Written by Richard Wentk, author of *The Which? Guide to Computers* and *The Which? Guide to the Internet*, this guide offers practical advice on choosing the best hardware and software for small businesses; finding training and support; getting free help before buying; how to avoid common computer problems.

Paperback   216 x 135mm   272 pages   £10.99

Available from bookshops, and by post from
Which?, Dept TAZM, Castlemead,
Gascoyne Way, Hertford X, SG14 1LH

You can also order using your credit card
by phoning FREE on (0800) 252100
(quoting Dept TAZM)